Managing Social Research

This book is an exceptional and essential _____ anyone planning to undertake social research. Tackling the specific concerns and issues that arise in conducting social research, *Managing Social Research* will especially benefit researchers working in a variety of different contexts, including those in academia, central or local government, public bodies, charities or private consulting companies. This well-structured text offers a comprehensive introduction to a range of important areas in project management, including:

- commissioning research
- preparing a tender or grant application
- risk and stakeholder analysis
- planning and scheduling a project
- managing the fieldwork and data analysis
- disseminating results
- ethics, confidentiality, copyright and data protection.

Managing Social Research provides a unique source of guidance for anyone seeking to commission, manage or carry out social research.

Roger Tarling is Professor of Social Research at the University of Surrey. His research interests cover crime and criminal justice, the voluntary sector, research management, statistical modelling and quantitative research methods.

Social Research Today
Edited by Martin Bulmer

The *Social Research Today* series provides concise and contemporary intro-
ductions to significant methodological topics in the social sciences. Covering
both quantitative and qualitative methods, this new series features readable
and accessible books from some of the leading names in the field and is aimed
at students and professional researchers alike. This series also brings together
for the first time the best titles from the old *Social Research Today* and
Contemporary Social Research series edited by Martin Bulmer for UCL Press and
Routledge.

Other series titles include:

Principles of Research Design in the Social Sciences
Frank Bechhofer and Lindsay Paterson

Social Impact Assessment
Henk Becker

The Turn to Biographical Methods in Social Science
edited by Prue Chamberlayne, Joanna Bornat and Tom Wengraf

Quantity and Quality in Social Research
Alan Bryman

Research Methods and Organisational Studies
Alan Bryman

Field Research
A Sourcebook and Field Manual
Robert G. Burgess

In the Field
An Introduction to Field Research
Robert G. Burgess

Qualitative Analysis
Thinking, Doing, Writing
Douglas Ezzy

Research Design (second edition)
Catherine Hakim

Measuring Health and Medical Outcomes
edited by Crispin Jenkinson

Methods of Criminological Research
Victor Jupp

Information Technology for the Social Scientist
edited by Raymond M. Lee

An Introduction to the Philosophy of Social Research
Tim May and Malcolm Williams

Research Social and Economic Change
The Uses of Household Panel Studies
edited by David Rose

Introduction to Longitudinal Research
Elisabetta Ruspini

Surveys in Social Research (fifth edition)
David de Vaus

Researching the Powerful in Education
edited by Geoffrey Walford

Researching Race and Racism
edited by Martin Bulmer and John Solomos

Martin Bulmer is Professor of Sociology at the University of Surrey. He is Director of the Question Bank (a WWW resource based at Surrey) in the ESRC Centre for Applied Social Surveys (CASS), a collaboration between the National Centre for Social Research (NatCen), the University of Southampton and the University of Surrey. He is also a Director of the department's Institute of Social Research, and an Academician of the Academy of Learned Societies for the Social Sciences.

Managing Social Research

A practical guide

Roger Tarling

Routledge
Taylor & Francis Group

LONDON AND NEW YORK

First published 2006 by Routledge
2 Park Square, Milton Park, Abingdon, Oxon OX14 4RN

Simultaneously published in the USA and Canada
by Routledge
270 Madison Ave, New York, NY 10016

Routledge is an imprint of the Taylor & Francis Group

© 2006 Roger Tarling

Typeset in Garamond by
Keystroke, Jacaranda Lodge, Wolverhampton
Printed and bound in Great Britain by
MPG Books Ltd, Bodmin, Cornwall

British Library Cataloguing in Publication Data
A catalogue record for this book is available from the British Library

Library of Congress Cataloging in Publication Data
A catalog record for this book has been requested

ISBN 0–415–35516–8 (hbk)
ISBN 0–415–35517–7 (pbk)

Contents

Illustrations

Tables

Figures

Preface

For more years than I care to remember I have been managing social research. I have led and directed many individual research projects and while at the Home Office Research and Planning Unit I formulated and managed programmes of research. As Head of RPU for six years I was closely involved in developing research strategies that could inform high-level policy objectives. I was also accountable for the RPU's multi-million pound research budget. My position also led to my membership of many professional committees and Working Groups deliberating on various aspects of research management and the issues that arise when conducting social research. Participation included membership of the ESRC Datasets Policy Working Group (which looked at the implications for social researchers of the law on copyright, confidentiality and data protection). I was also member of a team that prepared the British Society of Criminology Code of Research Ethics.

Since leaving the Home Office, I have been running courses on research management for social researchers, both at the University of Surrey (as part of its Day Course Programme) and for six years at the Civil Service College (for Government Social Researchers). I searched in vain for a suitable text to recommend to students but I found them to be either of the 'How to Write a PhD' variety or to be extremely dense texts on project management for the manufacturing, construction or IT industries. The latter genre did not include examples pertinent to social research and omitted topics that are paramount in it, such as, commissioning research, applying for funding, ethics, data protection and report writing. It is my view that managing social research does not warrant the level of sophistication or such in-depth analysis as is found in standard project management texts, but that social researchers would benefit from greater awareness of project management principles suitably adapted for their circumstances. In the end I could resist Martin Bulmer's pressure no longer and wrote my own text book. This is the result.

The aim of this book is to describe the process of social research and the stages from the inception to the completion of a project. The book is essentially about the science and art of managing social research, a skill that is becoming increasingly important to complement theoretical knowledge and skills in research design and methodology.

The book is intended as a practical manual and guide for all levels of student who are studying research or conducting research as part of their course. It is also intended to be of benefit to the many thousands of people who are pursuing social research careers in academia, government and other public bodies and agencies, the voluntary and private sectors.

Acknowledgements

I was encouraged to write this book by my colleague at the University of Surrey, Martin Bulmer. But I could not have written it without the support of others. Many friends and colleagues have taught me so much about various aspects of project management; some of them have presented on courses that I have run. I am truly indebted to: John Burrows, Janet Gawn, Stephen Jones, Keith Kirby, Jeremy Neathey, Joan Payne, Simon Prager, Steve Shaljean-Tilley and William Solesbury. I would especially like to thank Martin, Janet, Keith and Stephen, who kindly read early drafts of sections of this book and provided many useful comments and Annie Tarling who helped in the preparation of the manuscript.

I would also like to express my appreciation to the Office of the Deputy Prime Minister for allowing me to reproduce both their guidance on preparing a specification of requirement and an example of one prepared within the department. I am also grateful to Jonathan Brown, Wales Council for Voluntary Action, for allowing me to reproduce specification of requirement prepared by him.

I am grateful to the ESRC for permission to adapt and update its 'Guidelines on copyright and confidentiality: legal issues for social science researchers' in the preparation of Chapter 10.

Despite the contribution of others, unfortunately I cannot blame anyone but myself for any errors or omissions found in this book.

1 Introduction

The recent Commission on the Social Sciences (2003) found it difficult, if not impossible to define social science other than in the broadest terms. 'In essence, then, we have come to see the social sciences as about "disciplined curiosity about societies in which we all live", leading to the creation and sharing of social knowledge.' The Commission felt the term social science was a misnomer 'given the huge range of interests, ways of operating, research methodologies and value systems extant' and had no alternative but to adopt a working definition based on the academic disciplines. The Economic and Social Research Council recognises sixteen disciplines as falling within its remit: area studies; economic and social history; economics; education; environmental planning; human geography; interdisciplinary studies; linguistics; management and business studies; political studies and international relations; psychology; social anthropology; social policy; socio-legal studies; sociology; and statistics, computing and methodology. This classification could be endlessly debated. Where does criminology fall within this schema, and could certain aspects of health care be seen as social rather than medical? Nevertheless, the list does serve to illustrate the breadth and diversity of social science.

If social science is difficult to define because of its heterogeneity, it is not surprising that social research comes in many different shapes and sizes, involving a wide variety of approaches and methodologies. However, a brief description of a not untypical research project that I undertook will help to illustrate the generic issues that arise when managing any social research project. The project was an evaluation of the Dalston Youth Project (a full account can be found in Tarling *et al.*, 2001).

The Dalston Youth Project (DYP) was conceived to work with young people aged between 11 and 14 who were defined to be 'at risk' of dropping out of school and of becoming involved in offending behaviour. It planned to offer them some support during the formative period of early adolescence and to direct them towards a more socially acceptable and safer lifestyle.

The four aims of the project were:

1   to improve basic education skills (literacy, numeracy, life skills) in the target group as well as to increase the group's motivation to learn
2   to improve social skills and reduce conflict with parents and other adults
3   to reduce offending rates, drug use, truanting or other at-risk behaviour within the target group
4   to establish a team of volunteers in the local community trained and supported by the project to act as mentors to the young people.

There were four main strands to the programme:

Residential weekend This took place at an activity centre at the beginning of the project. Young people and mentors attended, providing an opportunity to meet and identify with the project. The demanding activities were intended to build confidence and self-esteem.

Mentoring component Each young person was paired with a volunteer mentor. Mentors offered guidance and emotional support as well as providing a positive role model.

Educational component Each young person was given six hours of tuition after school during term time, to help develop numeracy and literacy skills.

Parent/guardian component The support and involvement of parents/guardians was seen as vital, home visits were arranged and parenting skills sessions were organised.

Thirty young people were placed on the programme for one school year, ten from each of three nearby 'feeder' schools. The project received initial funding for three years, so three cohorts of thirty young people were recruited to the project. The research project assessed the development of DYP during its inception and its first three years of operation.

The number of staff running the project varied slightly during the three years, but mainly comprised a full-time project manager, three part-time tutors, a part-time mentoring coordinator and some part-time administrative support staff. Oversight of DYP and the evaluation research project was provided by a Steering Committee, comprising representatives of the sponsor (the Home Office), the schools, the local education department and the local youth service, the police, the project staff and the research team. The evaluation team consisted of three researchers, all of whom worked part-time on the evaluation.

The research comprised a process evaluation, describing how DYP evolved and developed, and an impact evaluation, assessing the extent to which the DYP achieved its aims and objectives.

A multi-method approach to data collection was adopted and included:

- a review of the literature produced by DYP describing the programme
- attendance at Steering Committee meetings and 'awaydays'
- semi-structured interviews with members of DYP staff
- non-participant observation at the residential weekend, mentor training sessions and other activities organised by DYP
- classroom observations of the educational classes
- semi-structured interviews and conversations with young people, mentors and parents/guardians
- site visits to the participating schools
- extraction of information from DYP, school and police records
- administering literacy and numeracy tests and self-completion self-esteem questionnaires.

From this description of the Dalston Youth Project and the evaluation, several key points emerge which are generic to most social research to some degree or other.

First, there are many stakeholders with very differing interests in the project. Many were represented on the Steering Committee (the sponsor, the schools, the local education department and the local youth service, the police, the project staff and the research team). Other important stakeholders included the young people themselves, their parents/guardians and the mentors.

Second, because of the many aspects to the methodology and the nature and timing of the activities in DYP, the evaluation had to be carefully planned and scheduled. To take an obvious example, the residential weekend could only be observed when it took place. Evaluation team members had specific responsibilities which had to be taken into account when devising the schedule of work. Progress of the evaluation had to be monitored constantly.

Third, there were risks to the research, principally that key stakeholders, the young people, would not participate in the evaluation.

Fourth, a considerable amount of time (and skill) was involved in negotiation, not to overcome any ill-will, but simply because of the number of individuals and agencies involved.

Fifth, research with any subjects, but particularly with young people, raises many ethical issues, such as of informed consent, confidentiality and so on. These have to be addressed and resolved.

Sixth, steps were needed to ensure relevant, useful and reliable data of a sufficient quality was collected.

Aim of the book

It is a reality that anyone who joins the social research community or makes a career of social research will, at some stage, be involved in defining, designing, undertaking or communicating research. Over time the social researcher may act as an intelligent customer to help policy makers, practitioners or funders identify gaps in knowledge and research need. Having diagnosed research need the researcher may be tasked with procuring research and with appointing contractors to undertake it and be asked to review and make judgements on research proposals. On other occasions the researcher will be the research supplier or part of the team that is funded to carry out the work – namely to design and manage the project, collect and analyse the data. Whether sponsor or supplier, throughout the period of the research project and certainly at the conclusion, the findings will need to be reported and disseminated to a variety of different audiences.

The aim of this book is to describe the process of social research and the stages from the inception to the completion of a project. It considers the issues that need to be addressed at each stage, the practices that have been, or might need to be, adopted and the skills required. The book is essentially about the science and art (for it is a mixture of both) of managing social research, a topic which is neglected in most formal educational Research Methods courses, and yet it is a skill that is becoming increasingly important to complement theoretical knowledge and skills in research design and methodology.

Project management is a well-developed subject in its own right and is applied extensively, if not routinely, in the construction, manufacturing and IT industries, and the government too has developed its own project management protocol, PRINCE. A large body of literature is available describing the techniques and procedures that have been developed. A good text of this genre is Field and Keller (1998), which provides greater depth and insights for those who feel they need to know more. However, it is 441 pages in length and yet does not cover all the issues that may be relevant in social research. The view taken here is that managing social research does not warrant this level of sophistication or such in-depth analysis but that social researchers would benefit from greater awareness of project management principles suitably adapted for their circumstances. Furthermore, there are issues (data protection, confidentiality, report writing and dissemination) which require more attention in social research than in other areas like construction, for example. These topics are given more prominence in this book.

Plan of the book

The book is structured to follow the broad sequence of events in undertaking research, from commissioning to writing a report and disseminating the findings. However, there are two limitations to following this schema. First, undertaking research is not an altogether straightforward sequence of activities with one activity beginning when one ends. For example, much of the final report can be written early in the project life cycle. Second, many issues need to be kept under constant review, for example risk, planning and staff management, do not simply arise at one point during the project where they are dealt with and concluded. Nevertheless, books are laid out sequentially and the material of this book has to conform, so while most topics are dealt with as they occur in the project cycle, others, which do not conform to this neat chronology, are interspersed at points that seem most appropriate.

The remainder of this chapter sets the context by defining basic terms, describing the size and structure of what might be called the UK social research industry and by setting out the legal framework in which social researchers operate.

Definitions of project, research and management

If the subject of the book is managing research projects, let us begin by defining those terms. They are considered in reverse order.

Project

> A project is a defined piece of work, undertaken for somebody within an agreed timescale and budget, using specific resources for a specific purpose.

This definition draws out the essential features of a project in that a project is a discrete, usually one-off, activity, bound by time and resources. It is undertaken with a particular aim in mind. The three essential parameters of any project are time, cost/resources and quality and in most projects, there is a trade-off between them. Additional resources and/or more time may lead to higher quality, but time and resources are not infinite (and better quality does not always accrue simply from more effort – or a ceiling is reached beyond which additional effort brings only marginal improvements in quality).

Thus when embarking on a project it is imperative to be absolutely clear:

- of the project's aims and purpose (including the quality standard it is expected to attain);
- who the customer for the project is (which of course may be the researcher);
- the timescale and the resources available.

These three points cannot be emphasised too strongly as they set the boundary and the constraints within which one is working. Of course, any of these parameters may change during the course of a project and it may even be desirable to change some of them if more time or additional resources are required to complete the project. But if this is the case it should be anticipated, planned and negotiated. The project should not simply be allowed to drift unnecessarily over budget or over time through lack of appropriate action.

The criteria for assessing whether a project is or has been successful stem directly from the definition. They can be stated thus:

- to specification
- on time
- within budget
- to quality.

The first three do not require elaboration, however, a word on quality. Quality is defined as *fitness for purpose* which at first sounds tautological and unhelpful but does serve to emphasise that quality is a relative not an absolute concept. It is as well to be aware of this when specifying or judging research. If the initial purpose of the research project was to 'provide some insights' or 'gain an impression of' it should not be judged adversely retrospectively because it did not achieve a certain level of precision of measurement. And a project should not be continued solely to achieve a quality standard not originally specified.

A project can be judged to have failed if it fails to meet any one of the four criteria of success listed above.

Projects are said to have four distinct phases:

1   conceiving and defining the aims and objectives of the project
2   planning the project
3   implementing the project according to the plan
4   concluding the project and disseminating the results.

While these four phases serve to emphasise the broad progress of a project and to highlight the different skills that might be needed at each phase, in social research projects the boundaries between each phase are not always so clear-cut.

Research

The Higher Education Funding Council for England (HEFCE) defines research as

> *original* investigation undertaken in order to gain knowledge and under-standing.

For the purpose of producing Government SET (science, engineering and technology) statistics, research and development is taken to include *creative* work undertaken on a systematic basis in order to increase the stock of knowledge, including knowledge of man, culture and society, and the use of this stock of knowledge to devise new applications.

Original in the first definition and *creative* in the second have been emphasised here to underscore the distinctive nature of research. Each research project is different. It may bear some similarities to previous projects, especially where its purpose is to replicate earlier work, and most methodologies are tried and tested. Nevertheless, the investigator, the setting, the context and the subjects are invariably different. Because of the uncharted nature of certain elements of each research project 'expect the unexpected'. Research projects usually take a good deal longer to complete than originally anticipated. To be forewarned is to be forearmed, when planning research allow additional time to deal with the unexpected that will inevitably arise.

From my own experience I recall that the first British Crime Survey took the best part of five years from conception in 1977 to completion in 1982. The first BCS was very much a research project breaking new ground (although there had been an earlier, smaller-scale victim survey in England and several victim surveys in the USA). A good deal of time was taken up in defining the aims of the project, liaising with stakeholders, designing and testing the survey (in particular the questionnaire) and in securing the funding. Once the first BCS had been satisfactorily completed, subsequent surveys had an increasingly well-trodden path to follow and are now conducted continuously and routinely every year.

Management

The Oxford English Dictionary defines managing

> as the application of skill or care in the manipulation, use, treatment or control (of things or persons) or in the conduct (of an enterprise, operation etc.).

The industrialist Henri Fayol writing in 1916 was one of the first to attempt a definition of management. He defined it as the process of

> forecasting, planning, organising, commanding, coordinating, and controlling.
>
> (as quoted in Pettinger, 1994)

There have been other definitions since Fayol's, which use different terminology (for example, directing for commanding), but his definition has stood the test of time. Certainly all the main functions that a manager is expected to perform are included. It is often said in management texts that management is the same whether one is managing the school fete or a multinational company. These authors have obviously never managed a school fete. The principles might well be the same but there is an important difference between the two in that those involved in the school fete are not employees but volunteers who can quit if they do not like a decision. The parallel with social research is that we are often expecting research subjects to participate voluntarily in projects.

Starting with a clear vision of what is to be achieved – an essential prerequisite – a *plan* is required in order that the necessary tasks are done in the right order. *Planning* also involves forecasting events and the level of resources needed.

Once the project is underway, the manager will be required to *organise* and *coordinate* the work – deciding who does what when and how, assigning and delegating tasks as appropriate.

Commanding and *directing* does not only imply instructing but also motivating and leading the team.

It is also extremely important to keep *control* of the project to ensure that everything is going according to plan, on time and within budget. If not, remedial action will be needed.

In order to discharge the functions outlined above, a manager requires a range of specific skills.

First, the manager will need *analytical skills*, to understand what progress is being made and to identify and resolve any problems that occur.

Second, the manager will need *communication* and *influencing* skills, to promote the project, to engage stakeholders, to lead and motivate the team and to disseminate the findings of the research.

Third, the manager will need *decision-making* skills, to keep the project on track and to avoid delay and drift.

Note the inclusion of the words *skill* and *care* in the Oxford Dictionary definition. Although skills can be learned and developed, care (consideration, thoughtfulness, tact and sensitivity) are also the hallmarks of a good manager as well as the ability to take decisive action.

Above all a manager must assume overall responsibility and invest sufficient (which often means considerable) time to managing the project. The manager cannot abdicate his or her responsibilities or expect the project to be managed in his or her absence.

Social research in the UK

It is impossible to arrive at an exact estimate of the size of social research industry in this country, either in terms of the number of people involved or in the monetary value of that activity, but by any standards it is both large and competitive. Writing in the late 1990s, Bulmer and Sykes (1998) guess-estimated the annual spend on social research to be as much as £600 million and employing between 10,000 and 20,000 people. Engagement in social research can be found in the following sectors, which have been grouped according to whether that sector funds research, conducts research or both – a mixture of the two.

Sponsors of research
- the Research Councils (mainly the Economic and Social Research Council (ESRC), but to a lesser extent the Arts and Humanities Research Council (AHRC) and the Medical Research Council (MRC)
- European Union (EU)
- industry and commerce.

Sponsors and suppliers of research
- higher education institutions
- government departments
- local and regional authorities, including health authorities and trusts
- quangos (quasi non-governmental organisations) or NDPBs (non-departmental public bodies)
- charities.

Suppliers/contractors of research
- non-profit research institutes
- market research companies
- private consultancy companies
- independent researchers
- professional associations and trade unions.

The taxonomy can only be approximate but does serve the purpose of identifying the leading players and the nature of their involvement in social research. The UK research councils, in particular the ESRC, and the EU only fund research. Private companies may also sponsor some social science research (in addition to market or consumer research undertaken in pursuit of their own corporate interests).

A large group are both funders and suppliers of social research. Academics may receive direct financial support or, more likely, indirect support from their higher education institutions. Most major government departments have internal social research units, which sponsor research in response to policy needs and agendas as well as conducting research 'in-house'. The arrangements in Local Authorities and quangos mirror those in central government departments, although usually on a smaller scale. The voluntary sector is rather different. Most charities exist to offer support and deliver services and seek funds themselves to pursue their objectives. However, other charities and philanthropic trusts give grants but few specifically fund social research (rather more sponsor medical research). The main foundations sponsoring social research are Joseph Rowntree, Leverhulme, Nuffield and, in Scotland, the Carnegie Trust. More information on funders of social research is provided in Chapter 4.

In addition to the many academics and university departments undertaking social research, suppliers include many of the large market research companies and large private consultancy firms. A growth in recent years has been in the number of smaller organisations that have grown up specialising in social research. These may be individuals acting as sole traders or small partnerships comprising a group of researchers. Non-profit research institutes are also well-established and significant players.

While it is not possible to measure the exact size of the social research industry some indicators are available. Each year the Higher Education Statistics Agency collates information from universities and other HE institutions on their income from research disaggregated by subject area (HESA, 2003). Grouping individual subject areas into those that fall within social research, the breakdown set out in Table 1.1 is obtained.

Table 1.1 Higher education institutions' funding for social science research: by source of funding

Source of funding	Funding £m	Percentage
Research Councils	52	22
UK charities	38	16
Government (central, local and health trusts)	100	42
Industry and commerce	14	6
European Union	16	7
Other overseas	11	5
Other	8	3
Total	239	100

Source: Higher Education Statistics Agency (HESA) (2003)

It can be seen that HE institutions received £239 m in 2001–02 to conduct social research. This income came mainly from government sources, with the research councils and charities also contributing sizeable amounts. Private companies, the EU and other overseas sponsors were much less prominent.

Table 1.1 offers only a partial insight, that is funds going to one supplier – namely academic institutions. Further insight can be gained by viewing social research from the funders perspective. The research councils are only permitted to fund HE institutions and reputable non-profit research organisations and the ESRC spends around £68 m per year on social research. The government is not so constrained, it can fund whoever it feels is most able to undertake the work. Information on central government's funding of social research is forthcoming from the Office for National Statistics (ONS) annual Government R&D Survey. Data for 2000–01 indicates that central government departments spent £270 m R&D money on 'social development and services' (OST, 2003). From Table 1.1 it would appear that £100 m went to HE institutes, leaving

£179 m to commission other research suppliers. However, a qualification is required, as some of this money will have been spent in supporting internal research and transfers between departments. For example, the Office for National Statistics will conduct large social surveys on behalf of other government departments, such as the British Crime Survey for the Home Office.

These indicators give credence to Bulmer and Sykes' (1998) estimates of the turnover of social research in this country of £600 m. Their estimate of 10,000–20,000 employees, however, may need revising upwards. In the 2001 Research Assessment Exercise (RAE) approximately 12,000 staff in social science disciplines in higher education institutions were reported as being 'research active' and there are a further 5,000 research students in the HE sector. In addition, there are approaching 1,000 Government Social Researchers employed in central government and a similar number of both economists and statisticians. There are also around 300 psychologists employed in government. However, not all of these professionals will be involved in social research and there may be an element of double counting between the groups. It is more difficult to estimate the numbers working in other sectors but the Social Research Association has about 700 members who are neither in academia nor GSR, but in market research, local government, the health service or the charity/voluntary sector. The figures given above only include professional staff, not the many other people who offer administrative and other support, or who are employed as interviewers for survey companies. Nevertheless, and despite the imperfections of measurement, at the present time a figure of between 20,000 and 30,000 engaged in social research seems nearer the mark.

Legal and ethical framework

Research, like any activity of human endeavour, is conducted within a legal and ethical framework. Social researchers need to be aware of the legislation governing and constraining research and of the ethical principles developed by professional associations and funders of research. Often the two coincide. What is seen to be ethical practice is also enshrined in law, for example, maintaining confidentiality and data protection. But ethical principles may impinge on activity, which is not illegal. Examples here would be giving full recognition to research assistants for their contribution to the project, or giving feedback to research participants, both of which are not legal requirements but would be seen by most as good ethical practice.

In describing relevant law and the codes that set ethical standards, some duplication is inevitable given the overlap between the two. This duplication is necessary in order to deal systematically and comprehensively with both. Ethics is the subject of Chapter 11. The first part summarises the ethical dilemmas that researchers often face and the approach to them recommended by professional bodies. The second part deals with the contentious issue of deciding who should make ethical decisions and who should be the final arbiter of them.

Major aims of legislation in liberal Western democracies are to protect human rights and to promote equality of opportunity, and these aims are as relevant when undertaking research as in any other aspect of life.

The Human Rights Act 1998

The Human Rights Act brings into UK law the Human Rights Convention. The Convention sets out a person's basic rights, such as a right to life, liberty and security, fair treatment under the law and respect for private and family life. It also sets out certain freedoms, including freedom of thought, conscience and religion and expression, as well as prohibiting certain acts, such as torture, slavery and discrimination. At present it is not clear what specific implications the Act has for social research in this country but it does reinforce in law high standards of conduct. The Act applies to action by 'public authorities' so research undertaken on behalf of government, local government or other public bodies is particularly within the compass of the HRA. In time legal challenges through the courts may impact on the way researchers can conduct research or engage with research participants, but there are no relevant court rulings to report at present. Researchers can keep abreast of developments by accessing the HRA website at www.dca.gov.uk/hract/. All relevant amendments to the law will be reported there.

Freedom of Information Act 2000

The Freedom of Information Act places an obligation on public bodies to make information available. Specifically, the Act conveys two statutory rights on citizens:

- to be told whether or not the public authority holds that information, and if so
- to have that information communicated to them.

Like the HRA, the Freedom of Information Act applies to the actions of public authorities so is most pertinent for publicly sponsored research. The Act also shares other similarities with the HRA in that it has only relatively recently come into effect (January 2005) and its impact has yet to be fully determined. There are grounds for thinking that its impact on social research may not be great as one exemption from disclosing information is if the information requested is 'intended for future publication' (section 22). Government sponsored social research is invariably published so the Act will not affect existing practice. In time, however, the Act might affect the speed of publication or the kind of information that needs to be recorded in a published report. In particular, it may lay down guidelines regarding how the research is to be described and reported. In addition, original data could be requested. Information about the research commissioning process could also be requested under FOI, including information about successful and unsuccessful proposals, the decision making process and the contract awarded to the successful contractor.

Researchers can find out more, as well as keeping up with developments, by consulting the Department of Constitutional Affairs website at www.dca.gov. uk/foi.

Equal opportunities and discrimination

Various acts either promote equal opportunities or prohibit discrimination. The Human Rights Act, which reasserts certain principles, has already been mentioned. Many of the acts outlined below relate in particular to 'fairness' in employment or in the provision of services. However, in spirit, if not always in law, the acts extend equally to the conduct of research and to the researcher's stance towards the subjects or participants of research.

The Sex Discrimination Act 1975 makes it unlawful to discriminate on the grounds of sex. Specifically, sex discrimination is not allowed in employment, education, advertising or when providing housing, goods, services or facilities.

Similarly, The Race Relations Act 1976, as amended by the Race Relations (Amendment) Act 2000, makes it unlawful to discriminate against anyone on grounds of race, colour, nationality (including citizenship), or ethnic or national origin. The amended Act also imposes general duties on many public authorities to promote racial equality.

The Equal Pay Act 1970 says women must be paid the same as men when they are doing equal work, and vice-versa.

The Disability Discrimination Act 1995 prohibits discrimination against persons with disabilities, and goes further by placing a statutory duty on employers and service providers to make 'reasonable changes' to the place of work and employment practices or, in the case of service providers, in the way services are delivered, so as not to cause discrimination. The DDA affects all employers and service providers so social researchers need to ensure their employment procedures conform and that they have made 'reasonable changes'. In addition, the Act has implications for the conduct of research and for planning and carrying out a study. Researchers need to ensure that people with disabilities are not excluded from participating in the research simply because of their disability. Can they attend focus groups or interviews or is that made difficult because of transport, wheelchair access to buildings, etc.? Has adequate provision been made for them to hear interviewers or read questionnaires?

Further details can be obtained from the website of the Equal Opportunities Commission (www.eoc.org.uk). Of particular interest is the EOC's helpful guidance contained in a series of 'checklists' on specific topics such as managing flexible working, pregnancy and maternity, sexual harassment, recruitment and selection. The Commission for Racial Equality provides helpful information at its website, www.cre.gov.uk. Guidance on what are 'reasonable changes' under the Disability Discrimination Act and the effects of recent amendments can be found at www.disability.gov.uk.

Although it has not yet come into law, the government has adopted the EU Directive on Equal Treatment. This Directive requires all EU countries to introduce legislation prohibiting direct and indirect discrimination at work on the grounds of age, sexual orientation, religion and belief and disability. As outlined above, laws are in place, which deal with most of these areas. The government is currently consulting on how to frame legislation, which prohibits discrimination on grounds of age.

A further development on the horizon is the government's proposal to replace the three existing commissions which safeguard rights and promote good practice on race, equal opportunities and disability (The Commission for Racial Equality, The Equal Opportunities, and the Disability Rights Commission) by one single Commission on Equality and Human Rights. It is not clear when this new body will come into being but it will not be before late 2006.

Welsh Language Act 1993

Social researchers need also to be aware of the requirement to comply with the Welsh Language Act. The implication under this act is that studies conducted in Wales should make provision for Welsh language translations or interpreters where appropriate. In practice this means that initial contacts to possible research subjects in Wales should be issued in Welsh and English and that should they wish, subsequent participation can be conducted in Welsh (for example, an interview conducted in Welsh or a questionnaire written in Welsh).

It is only Welsh that a legal obligation exists but similar consideration should be given to other groups for whom English may be a second language. Not only does this constitute good ethical practice but may be essential for the conduct, quality and validity of the research with certain groups of research subjects.

Employment law

In addition to the law mentioned above, which promotes equal opportunities and prohibits discrimination in employment, employment law also addresses other issues including what it means to be employed and the obligations it places on both employers and employees. There are also issues around safety at work and the responsibility of employers to have regard to the well-being of their staff. From an ethical standpoint, research managers will want to ensure that research assistants do not face undue risks in carrying out research regardless of whether they are employees or engaged on some other form of contract. Employment law and safety at work are considered in detail in Chapter 7.

Contract law

While a good deal of social research is conducted 'in-house' (by employees carrying out research on behalf of their employer or by academics working to their own agendas without external support), a considerable amount is commissioned by a funding body entering into a contract with a research supplier. Negotiating and drawing up contracts is a skill that social researchers require. The tendering process is discussed in Chapter 3 while negotiation is the subject of Chapter 5.

Copyright, confidentiality and data protection

Empirical social research involves interviewing or collecting background information on individual human subjects or organisations. There is a legal duty to treat the information disclosed confidentially, and the Data Protection Act (1998) imposes further stipulations on how the data must be handled. Furthermore, the research instruments, the data collected, any analyses and reports emanating from the research will confer copyright on their authors who might be the research subjects, the researchers, the funders or the publishers of the final products. All three topics are comprehensively dealt with in Chapter 10.

2 Stakeholder and risk analysis

Two important functions of a research manager's role are to manage stakeholders and to manage risks. Research managers are often reluctant to undertake these functions formally or to devote sufficient time to them. The view taken may be that neither are particularly interesting or important, certainly compared with the more intellectually stimulating aspects of the project. In the case of risks, the view is perhaps taken that they may not materialise and can be addressed if and when they do. This view is short sighted. The interests, perceptions and engagement of stakeholders should be kept under constant and continuous review. Similarly all possible and potential risks and problems that could occur to disrupt the project in any way should be anticipated and steps implemented to avoid or minimise those risks. Such investments will pay dividends.

Throughout this book reference will be made to stakeholders and to risks and the need to carryout a stakeholder analysis or a risk assessment analysis. Both are the subject of this chapter and are described here.

Stakeholder analysis

'Stakeholders are any persons (or groups) who have an interest in your project, are affected by it or who can influence its outcome' (Field and Keller, 1998).

Stakeholders can therefore be sponsors of the project, providing the vital resources to undertake the work. They may be policy makers or practitioners, or the end users of the research findings who have an interest in the outcome and its implications. Stakeholders can be the gatekeepers to the data or facilitators to the research subjects and thereby vital to the viability of the project. They may be the subjects of the research who will participate but who might ultimately be the beneficiaries of the research if it leads to developments in policy and practice that affects their lives. The general public (and the media as communicators of the findings to them) may also have an interest in the research and, of course, there will be other researchers or the academic community in general that will be keen to learn from the research. Last, but by no means least, those working on the project (the research team or other partners in a consortium) will have a stake in the project.

Obviously any one person or group of persons or organisations can be a stake-holder in more than one of the ways described above. Similarly their position may change throughout the life of a project.

It is also important to be aware that stakeholders can adopt different stances to the research or may have different attitudes towards it. Some may be enthusiastic supporters or champions keen to promote the research while others may feel threatened by the research as it may be perceived as enquiring critically into their practices or the quality of the service they provide. Some who might be tasked to assemble information for the researchers (get out files, produce databases and so on) may have little interest but just see the research as leading to additional burdens and additional demands on their time. While some will accord the research high priority others will see it as low priority, to be involved with only if time permits. To the researchers the project is perhaps the most salient aspect of their working lives on which their careers are built. Do not assume that all stakeholders will regard the project in the same light. The Drug Treatment Programmes for Offenders example, which is used to illustrate project planning in Chapter 6, involved collaboration with prisons and hence the support of prison governors. The prison governors were very supportive but our research had to take its place, and rightly so, behind more pressing matters of prison security and prisoners' welfare. As one governor put it, 'no governor gets sacked for not collaborating with research but they do if there is a riot or prisoners escape'.

Five steps in a stakeholder analysis

1 *Identify all stakeholders*

Several brainstorming sessions amongst the team, or discussions with the commissioner or other stakeholders may be required to identify everyone who needs to be classified as a stakeholder. For each stakeholder a record should be made of their relation to the project, in essence what makes them a stakeholder.

2 *Identify each stakeholders' contribution to the project*

What does the project need from the stakeholder? It may just be support or goodwill or it may be more tangible, in terms of time, resources, specific information, etc.

3 *Estimate the impact of the project on each stakeholder*

At a practical or logistical level, will the project cause disruption to existing schedules? More significantly, could the findings of the research lead to major changes in the lives of certain stakeholders?

4   *Consider each stakeholders' power to influence the project*

Is the stakeholders' position (and the power that stems from it) such that they can cause delays (or hasten progress) to the project? Are their powers such as to be able to change the direction of the project, or worse, close it down, or more positively, expand it? Some stakeholders may have no power to exert, although most have, if only at the margins or indirectly.

5   *Judge each stakeholders' attitude to the project*

Attitudes can change and one needs to judge past, present and future attitudes.

Action plan

The purpose of undertaking a stakeholder analysis is to assemble the information that will assist in managing stakeholders and hence aspects of the project itself. The analysis will reveal which stakeholders are key and in what way and at what point in the project. Some will be crucial to get the project off the ground while others will be required to provide access at the fieldwork stage and so on. The analysis should also help to reveal who may need to be informed of the project and who may still need to be won over. In the analysis it is an option to grade or weight any of the elements to determine, for example, whether the impact on a particular stakeholder can be regarded as 'high', 'medium' or 'low'. Adopting a formal scale can help target the most important stakeholders or the vital actions to take. In most situations such a formal procedure may not be necessary but whatever less formal systems are used the end result should be the same, namely to arrive at a plan of action to engage stakeholders.

The stakeholder analysis should therefore lead to an action plan or a communication plan setting out:

- who needs to be contacted
- when do they need to be contacted
- how they are to be contacted (phone call, face to face meeting, letter or email)
- who in the research team will be responsible for engaging with the stakeholder
- what issues are to be addressed in the communication/consultation.

A stakeholder analysis and the subsequent action that follows as a result of it is not a one-off exercise, it will need to be repeated periodically throughout the life of the project.

Risk assessment analysis

Like most activities in life, in every project there is an element of risk that events will not proceed according to plan. Some risks may delay the project, some may result in additional resources having to be found and some may be fatal in that they prevent the project from achieving its stated objectives. The purpose of a risk assessment exercise is to identify risks to the project, their likely impact or the consequences they may have for the project. Informed of the risks, it is the project manager's responsibility to take preventive action where possible to minimise the project's exposure to those risks and the impact of them.

While risk is invariably thought of as leading to problems which are to be avoided, it is as well to remember that risk stems from uncertainty and uncertainty can also lead to unanticipated positive opportunities. At the same time as guarding against the adverse consequences, the project manager also needs to spot the opportunities should they occur and capitalise upon them.

The answer to the question 'what can go wrong with a project?', is 'everything and something will'. However, it is not helpful to think in such general terms. A risk assessment is only useful if it identifies the risks in sufficient detail leading to a decision over the action that can be taken. So, for example, one identified general risk might be that the final report is not written. However, that risk is expressed in insufficient detail to suggest a course of action. It is far better to describe the risk in terms of 'what might lead the final report not to be written?' The answer to this question might be 'not sufficient time allocated', 'the person responsible does not have the expertise', or 'the person may have left the project'. Solutions to these problems can then be thought through and steps taken to guard against the adverse outcome.

Six steps in a risk assessment analysis

1 Identify risks to the project

Identify risks in sufficient detail to enable actions to be considered. The project team will be able to identify possible risks and it is a good idea to consult stakeholders who are often aware of risks that are not obvious to the project team. Another source of advice are other researchers who have undertaken research in the same substantive area or researchers who have particular experience of the methodology to be adopted.

2 Assess each risk in terms of its impact on the project

A risk can affect a project in several different ways. It may disrupt the timetabling and scheduling of the project, it may affect quality or it may lead to increased cost. Impact should be considered across all dimensions.

3   *Assess each risk in terms of the probability of its occurrence*

How likely is it that the risk will occur during the project? When could it occur? Answers to these two questions, which gauge the project's exposure to risk, are needed.

4   *Prioritise risks*

Risks can be ranked according to each of the two criteria, impact and probability. A simple scoring system could be used grading risks into 'high impact', 'medium impact' and 'low impact' and in terms of probability 'high likelihood', 'medium likelihood' and 'low likelihood'. Having graded the risks they can then be assembled in a two-way matrix with impact as the rows and probability as the columns. This is depicted in Table 2.1.

Table 2.1 Risk priority matrix

	High likelihood	*Medium likelihood*	*Low likelihood*
High impact	R2, R4		R5
Medium impact		R3	
Low impact	R6		R1

Those risks in the top left hand corner are risks of most concern as they have the highest chance of occurring and would have the greatest impact on the project. In the example two risks, R2 and R4, fall into this category and require the greatest attention. R5 is less likely to occur, but if it does it will have a significant impact. Conversely, R6 is very likely to occur but will have low impact. R3 has been graded medium on both dimensions and R1 low on both dimensions.

5   *Identify a course of action for each risk*

There are at least five different responses that can be contemplated. First, a risk might be *prevented* by not pursuing a particular element of a project. Steps can be taken to *reduce* the impact or likelihood of a risk. On occasion the impact of the risk can be *transferred* to a third party (insurance operates on this principal of transferring risk). A response to risk is a *contingency* plan that can be put into operation should the risk materialise. Finally, a risk might simply have to be *accepted*. Every project involves risks and the only true way to avoid them all is to abandon the project. If the project is to continue, some risks which cannot be guarded against will simply have to be accepted.

6 *Identify who takes responsibility for the action*

Having identified the risks and thought through the measures that need to be taken, it is important to designate who in the project team is to take responsibility for putting in place the appropriate action.

A risk log

In a large project it is customary to assemble all the information generated in the risk analysis into a formal risk log. The risk log would itemise the following information:

- the risk (a title and a description of the risk)
- impact
- probability
- time of occurrence
- response/action
- action date
- owner/person responsible for the action.

Even in small projects a risk log can be a useful document in aiding the management of the project. Furthermore, accumulating information by keeping a record of problems and responses in individual projects can turn into an invaluable reference source when embarking on future projects. Gaining knowledge and experience in project management is as important as gaining knowledge and research experience in a substantive topic area or of a particular methodology.

Note

Risks (like stakeholders) can change throughout a project. New risks may arise while others made fade during the course of a project. For example, the risk of not obtaining responses to a questionnaire will end when completed questionnaires have been returned, but new risks arise in the coding and analysis of the information. Individual risks can also be compounded to exacerbate other risks. For example, if delays occur at one point in a project it could jeopardise later stages of the project and thereby introduce additional risk. Furthermore, the opportunity for different responses to a risk may change throughout a project.

For all these reasons it is important to keep risks to the project under constant review. Like the stakeholder analysis described earlier, it is not a one-off exercise but an ongoing task for the project manager in particular.

What goes wrong with social research projects?

As mentioned before, the short answer to this question is that anything and everything can. Below is a list of the most common risks a social research project faces.

Problems which stakeholders create

- Sponsors have greater expectations of the research than the research is able to meet. This can create problems towards the end of a project when the conclusions are found to be equivocal or not in line with prior assumptions.
- The project lacks clear focus, possibly because the sponsors are tempted to set too many aims for the research. At best any one research project can only answer a relatively small number of research questions. The lack of focus may stem from an ill-prepared specification of requirement (see Chapter 3) or the research supplier not being sufficiently informed of the context or background to the research.
- Commissioners/funders of the research lose interest in the subject matter of the research part way through the project life-cycle. This may be because the policy agenda has moved at a greater pace than envisaged when the project was commissioned and decisions that the research was to inform have been taken. (A researcher once told me that she heard on a radio news bulletin that the government initiative that she was in the process of evaluating had been discontinued.) Other scenarios are that the instigator or champion for the project has moved to another job or other more pressing issues have arisen that need to be given higher priority.
- Inadequate funding and too little time are allocated to the project. Results are always wanted 'yesterday' (I was once asked by a minister if we could not complete a two-year follow-up study within six months) and there is always the pressure to cut costs. Inadequate provision is likely to exacerbate the problems highlighted in the first two bullet points above.
- Stakeholders (in particular practitioners and research subjects) view the project as threatening and are hostile towards it and refuse to cooperate. (It took a considerable time to reach agreement with the judiciary on a study examining sentencing practices.)
- Stakeholders lack interest and commitment and, through inertia rather than hostility, cause delays and disruptions to the project plan.
- Inadequate communication and dialogue takes place between stakeholders and researcher. This situation can have many different implications ranging from small changes to the original plan to substantial drift in focus.
- Long delays in reaching agreement over publication of the report occur, because the commissioner does not like, or does not agree with, the findings, or simply due to inertia on the part of the commissioner who has lost interest. At the extreme, the research may never be published.

Problems implementing the project

- There are delays in gaining access to data or to research subjects.
- Data is found to be inadequate. It is quite common to find when gathering data from administrative records that data is missing or has not been recorded.
- Some or all of the data is lost to the project – mislaid, stolen, corrupted (the equipment failed to record, the computer system was not backed up). Apart from the loss to the project, loss of data may lead to breaches of confidentiality or of the terms of any contract.
- The methodology adopted cannot answer the research questions. Leaving aside the appropriateness of the methodology chosen or technical issues concerning the methodology (both topics are outside the scope of this book), problems arise because the research question may be too difficult to answer, or because other extraneous or confounding factors cannot be adequately controlled or isolated. Another cause may be the lack of sufficient testing and piloting of the methodology or research instruments.
- There is a lack of appropriate quality assurance at the fieldwork stage (an issue discussed in more detail in Chapter 8).
- There is a breakdown in the effective functioning of the research team, especially when several researchers from different organisations are collaborating or working in a consortium to undertake the project. There can be several contributory factors, although it is not always clear what is cause and what effect. Different disciplinary backgrounds amongst team members can lead to tensions over approach or interpretation (or simply difficulty in communicating with each other). There may be a lack of contractual or line management controls. Frustrations, stresses and pressures may simply lead to clashes of personality. Any one project can only accommodate one, at most two egos. (An issue can also be a lack of communication between the team and the commissioner of the project, which was listed amongst the problems which stakeholders create – but of course the problem could be created by the research team.)
- Research suppliers take on too much work or have too many commitments (for example, other projects or teaching) resulting in insufficient time being devoted to the project.
- Insufficient attention is given to project management by the Principal Investigator/Research Manager/Team Leader who is not planning and monitoring progress or anticipating problems. The problem may stem from having too many other commitments, as identified in the previous point, but differs in that when researchers have sufficient time, they still may not accord project management the priority it requires nor have the analytic skills to monitor and control the project.
- The reports are inadequate, either targeted at the wrong audience or simply badly written. (Dissemination is addressed in Chapter 9.)

Of the large number of potential problems listed above, personally I find 'delays in gaining access to data or to research subjects' the most salient as it seems to occur in every project. Hence if I can offer one piece of advice it is to make every effort to facilitate access at the earliest possible opportunity. The consequences of delay at this stage are far-reaching and are felt throughout the rest of the project. Additional time gaining access eats into time allocated to collecting and analysing the data and writing the final report. It is not uncommon to have the data in a state ready for analysis only a few weeks before the project is due to end. The rush at the end to complete the project invariably means that the data are under-analysed and only 'headline' results are presented. The quality of the final report also suffers as a result.

Some delays cannot be avoided but many can be avoided or foreshortened by a little forethought and planning and by making approaches to the gatekeepers of the data as soon as is practically possible.

The most common complaint of funders of social research is the poor quality of the final product, especially the quality of the final written report. Government researchers commissioning research say that shifting priorities and policy agendas cause disruptions and handling difficulties for them. Government researchers need to stay in close touch with their internal policy partners in order to respond to the changing context for the research.

Example: Sport and Leisure Activities for Young People

Government funds have been allocated to support a major initiative to provide sport and leisure activities for young people during school holidays. A range of providers bid to run individual projects and forty were successful. The projects are spread across the country and include a wide variety of sporting, artistic and cultural activities. Providers also vary from local authorities, not-for-profit organisations to private companies. Some providers have teamed up with schools in order to make use of the school's facilities.

Three government departments have contributed towards the funding of the initiative, principally the Department for Sport and Leisure, the Department for Schools and the Ministry of the Interior. The Ministry of the Interior is particularly interested in the potential of the initiative to reduce offending by young people during school holidays. All three departments wish to evaluate the initiative and have provided funding for the evaluation. The evaluation has the following components:

- data collection from schemes on uptake, participation, etc.
- in-depth case studies of a small number of schemes
- quantitative survey of participants and projects workers

- a study of the crime reduction effects of the scheme
- a cost–benefit analysis.

It has not been possible to find one organisation that can undertake all the components of the project. The most promising tender is from a consortium of four organisations. In the lead is a university research centre specialising in research on young people, which will undertake the first two components. The other three include a well-known survey company, a criminology department from another university with a track record in evaluating crime reduction schemes, and, finally, a not-for-profit organisation specialising in economic analysis including cost–benefit analysis.

The project is to last eighteen months, but it must be completed on time in order that results can feed into a crucial stage of the policy process, which is to consider how the initiative might develop in the future.

This example is fictitious but draws on many real case studies. It has been constructed to be typical of many large evaluation studies involving several funders, different research organisations working collaboratively in a consortium and different groups of research participants. It is not the intention here to undertake a full-scale stakeholder and risk analysis but rather to draw out and illustrate salient issues that arise in such studies.

Stakeholders

A range of stakeholders for the project can be identified. These include:

- government departments (as both sponsors and as stakeholders interested in the implications of the results for policy development)
- local authority departments (leisure, education and schools, youth services, social services)
- art/sport/leisure organisations
- youth-related agencies
- local community representatives
- charities
- activity providers
- Youth Offending Teams (YOTs)
- police – local and national
- young people
- families/parents
- project team.

Risks

The major risks are:

- Are there too many aims and objectives for the project/can expectations be met?
- A large number of stakeholders – will they all commit?
- Are the project evaluation outputs clear/can a successful outcome be identified?
- Can the impact of the project be isolated from other extraneous events?
- Is the data available and of a suitable quality?
- Are there confidentiality and data protection issues arising from transferring data between agencies?
- Will the research teams collaborate effectively?
- Is the timescale realistic?

The first point to note is the large number and range of stakeholders, especially when it is recognised that each project will involve a different provider and be located in a different local authority area, each served by a different education authority, police force and so on. A *considerable* amount of time will need to be set aside to contact and negotiate with the many stakeholders.

The stakeholders will have different agendas and expectations. It is not easy to work with more than one sponsor – whoever they might be (and despite efforts to 'join up' government). To take another example, the Home Office may have a different perspective on school exclusions from the Department for Education and Skills. The former seeing exclusions as providing opportunities for criminal behaviour, and hence wishing the number imposed to be minimised, the latter regarding exclusions as a means of improving the quality of school life for the majority of pupils by removing the most disruptive. In the Sport and Leisure example the government departments may well have different policy agendas to purse and have different expectations as to how the research may advance those agendas.

There may well be jealousies and rivalries amongst the local organisations and local authority departments. Each will have an eye to the outcomes of the project and the implications of those outcomes to them. They may also wish to minimise their input to the evaluation, especially if this entails onerous provision of data.

The activity providers will wish the research to assess their endeavours in a favourable light and may well criticise any research findings that come to a different conclusion.

The involvement of many stakeholders will be to supply data. Will they be prepared to do so and will they be able to provide it at the level of detail required? Will the data be comparable across the projects, or will it be subject to varying definitions and recording practices? To take but one example, data on crime and criminal behaviour will be needed from the police. But even if they are willing to help (and they invariably are), can their data systems provide the data at the local area level required and what confidentiality/data protection issues need to be resolved? Will the activity providers release names of the young people participating if their criminal records are to be made available?

Unavailability of data and data of insufficient quality are risks to the project, but more generally, is the methodology capable of answering the research questions, enabling the project to meet its aims and objectives? A good deal of unrelated activity will be occurring at the same time as the project and it may be very difficult to identify a successful outcome to the project or to disentangle the impact of the project from the impact of other events. One of the greatest challenges to social research is to evaluate satisfactorily the impact of large national social programmes.

In this example I also have considerable anxiety about the ability of the groups making up the consortium to work harmoniously, productively and effectively. It is my experience that each party will wish to renegotiate their respective responsibilities and remit during the course of the project, especially when things start to go wrong or tensions rise. I have witnessed occasions where collaboration has broken down leaving the sponsor to manage each individual group, link their respective contributions together and even write the final report. If I were commissioning this project, leading it or merely a member of one of the groups, I would want to see strong and tight contractual and management controls and evidence that the groups can work effectively together.

3 Commissioning research

Much research (including all that sponsored by government departments) originates prescriptively where the customer has a need for information and seeks to appoint a researcher to undertake the work in order to meet that need. This chapter deals with the issues and processes of getting from the formulation of need to the identification of the research supplier. In this situation, the role of the in-house research professional is to act as intelligent customer – the person who translates the initial request for information into a research brief and who exercises judgement in selecting the eventual contractor. The in-house researcher will also need to have knowledge of the research supplier market – which organisations specialise in what types of research and which organisations have knowledge of particular substantive areas.

Some small organisations, or organisations unaccustomed to commissioning social research, may not have the in-house expertise and capability to prepare a research brief, identify potential suppliers or judge submitted proposals. If not, it may well be expedient to seek assistance from a suitable external expert as the contribution of professional judgement and experience will be invaluable in the decision-making process. An alternative, and often profitable, way forward, especially where the research may pose particular problems, is to initiate a dialogue with the research community. This could take the form of a meeting or workshop with those known to have expertise in the area.

Before proceeding to appoint a research supplier, professional judgement should be brought to bear in answering the following, often neglected, questions.

1 Is the information already available and is new additional research necessary to meet the need?
2 Is the information worth having? There is always a cost to research and not just a financial cost but a cost in time and resources – not to mention an opportunity cost of the alternative use of that resource.
3 Can the information be obtained from research? There are many questions one would like to have answers to, but research may not be the best means of providing those answers (for example, trying to evaluate the impact of

a small intervention when there is no prospect of obtaining good and reliable information about how things were before the intervention).

4   Is the research doable? Is the data available and can it be obtained? Will the subjects agree to participate in the research?
5   Is the research justifiable on ethical grounds? (Ethical issues are dealt with in more detail in Chapter 11.)

Competition

Having considered these five questions and been satisfied that further research is appropriate, the next step is to decide the procedures for appointing a research supplier. In particular whether a competition is the best way to proceed and, if so, the form that the competition should take. The ultimate objectives are to ensure that the work is completed to the required quality standard (fitness for purpose) and that the research represents value for money (that the same outcome could not have been achieved for less outlay). Although not an objective for the research, great importance is attached to the selection procedures and decision-making processes being open, fair and transparent, especially when public money is being spent. Furthermore, in all organisations there will be a degree of accountability for those taking the decisions and the procedures which they followed.

Social researchers and procurement specialists who are influential in determining the procedures for commissioning research have not always been in agreement over the rules and how they may be applied. This led the Social Research Association to set up a subcommittee to develop good practice guidance. Their report *Commissioning Social Research: a good practice guide* (SRA, 2002) contains much useful information. The SRA Guide makes the point that research is not a commodity it is a service and should not be subjected to the same procurement rules as if purchasing a commodity. That is true, but if the argument is extended to plead a special case for research it cuts little ice with procurement specialists who point out that it is common and accepted practice to run competitions for the delivery of complex services. Research may be different from widgets but it is not different from many other professional services. Nevertheless, as with any professional service, the fine detail of the requirement may not be clear at the outset and both parties (the commissioner and the research supplier) will need to work closely and cooperatively, if not collaboratively, throughout the duration of the project. Mutual respect, dialogue and effective working relations will need to be fostered. The procedures should be such to enable a supportive environment as a means of achieving a successful outcome to the project. More enlightened procurement specialists understand this; as one told me 'a contract is a relationship' and as the SRA report states, 'the contractual tail should not be allowed to wag the operational dog' (SRA, 2002).

Is a competition the best way to proceed? In some situations it may not be if there is an obvious supplier who may be the only one to have the expertise, experience or unique access to the data and/or to the methodology. In such a case it is wasteful of everyone's time, especially those included to 'make up the numbers' (and, some would argue, unethical too) to hold a competition when the outcome is known from the start. In other situations research may be a continuation of previous research and if the existing contractor has performed satisfactorily a continuation contract may be appropriate. A third consideration is cost or size of the project. Again there seems little point in implementing disproportionate, lengthy and costly procedures to arrive at a decision to spend a small sum of money. Most large funders of research will specify a threshold of around £10,000 and projects falling below this limit can be let without the need for competition. Even larger contracts can be let by them as 'single tenders' (without competition) although a strong case has to be made to justify this course of action.

Some form of competition is the preferred method for many funders. Moreover, for public bodies commissioning large-scale projects, competition is often required under EU procurement rules (details of which are given later in this chapter). The advantage of competition is that by providing the funder with a range of suppliers to choose from, it is most likely to achieve the twin objectives of obtaining the right supplier to undertake the research whilst achieving value for money. Competition also achieves the objective of openness and transparency by enabling various suppliers the opportunity to bid. Competition avoids customers being locked into monopolistic suppliers who become stale and complacent and potentially inefficient and costly.

However, the disadvantages of competition should also be recognised, principally the process itself is costly and time consuming. Costs are incurred by the commissioning body in running a competition and each organisation that bids will incur costs in preparing a proposal. The costs to the commissioning body can increase dramatically if it is seeking to commission many moderately sized research projects and each is the subject of a separate competition. For the supplier, it is estimated that the average cost of preparing a bid is in the order of £5,000. Competition can also be a disincentive to potentially good suppliers who may not wish to incur the costs of competing if the chances of success are so small (although this can be overstated as there is an element of risk of being unsuccessful after preparing a detailed proposal wherever one seeks research funding). A fresh competition may also disrupt continuity and jeopardise a successful ongoing productive relationship.

The strategy then is to maximise the benefits that competition brings whilst minimising the disadvantages. Competition can take various forms all of which balance the pros and cons in different ways and it is worth considering the alternatives before proceeding.

Forms of competition

Dedicated research centres

A competition may be run to identify a supplier who will then be guaranteed to receive a specific substantial level of funding over a fixed period, maybe five years, to undertake research to that value. The exact nature of the research to be undertaken is not predetermined but negotiated at fixed points throughout the contract.

Apart from the obvious advantage of avoiding endless competitions for individual pieces of work, the main advantage is that the centre can recruit and train staff in the knowledge that a certain level of work will be coming in. Dedicated research centres can be particularly useful in specialist or technical areas where there are an insufficient number of researchers with the required level of knowledge or expertise to draw on. In essence by having a guaranteed level of security and continuity, the centre has the opportunity to build capacity by investing in staff and developing appropriate expertise. In the past this approach was favoured by the then Department of Social Security primarily because few social researchers had knowledge and expertise in social security and pension provisions. The Department of Health still favours this arrangement spending about one third of its social research budget to support about sixteen dedicated social research units, such as the Thomas Coram Research Unit, the Centre for Health Economics, the National Institute for Social Work Research Unit and the Nursing Research Unit. The Department for Education and Skills has three, one dedicated to researching Adult Basic Skills.

The main disadvantage of a dedicated centre is that it is often difficult to schedule the work on both sides to produce an even flow of work throughout the period (that is, research need from the commissioner and the resources from the supplier). The dedicated research centre is not an option for small funders whose research need is not great and what need they have is intermittent or sporadic.

Framework agreements/research partnerships/call-off contracts

This form of competition and the relationship it entails between commissioner and supplier can take slightly different forms and nomenclature, but in essence the funder holds a competition amongst potential suppliers and those that are successful can be contracted for work over a fixed period without further competition. Unlike the dedicated research centre model no funding is guaranteed, the supplier may be invited to undertake several projects during the period, one or two or none at all. The advantage of this arrangement is that it avoids running a competition each time a moderately small project is wanted – usually projects below £50,000 (above that limit a separate competition has to be held). Agreements can be entered into with any number of suppliers and often a range, offering different areas of knowledge or skills and expertise, are included. This form of arrangement is considered useful and cost effective and many central government departments now have such arrangements in place. There is a fairly substantial cost in running the initial competition in which many organisations are invited to bid, but this can be justified if it produces savings (on both sides) over the period. A potential disadvantage is that it tends to prevent new suppliers getting a foot in the door for the duration of the agreement.

Research programmes

Many individual projects are a continuation of a previous study, or complementary or related to other projects. In such circumstances it may be beneficial to group the projects and to run a competition for the projects collectively – wrapped up as a programme of research in a particular area. This can minimise costs for both commissioner and supplier. Of course the whole body of research need not go to the same supplier. The process of the competition can be used to decide who does which individual elements of the programme of work.

Individual research projects

The majority of research is, and probably always will be, commissioned on a project-by-project basis.

Preparing a specification of requirement

Having decided on the form the competition will take, and before the competition can be held, a brief, or specification of requirement, has to be prepared outlining the research that is needed. The specification of requirement (SoR) (also known as the Invitation to Tender (ITT)) is a key document in that it translates a broad requirement of the intended work into a more detailed and precise description of what is wanted. If the specification is not right there is little chance (or certainly less chance) of a satisfactory outcome to the research project. It is impossible to write a good specification without understanding fully what is wanted and if the writer is not clear he or she will not be able to convey that to prospective contractors in the specification.

In many commissioning organisations the general need for the project may have been identified some time before (and probably then only expressed or recorded in the most general terms). Time may have elapsed during which period the context for the research may have changed. It is also common that the individual tasked with preparing the specification is not the ultimate customer or consumer of the research. Before putting pen to paper (or fingers to keyboard) it is sound advice to consult with those who may have directly requested the project or who may have a role to play in it, that is, undertake a stakeholder analysis and consult with those identified in that analysis. It is also useful to undertake a risk analysis at this stage and to address possible risks to the project with those consulted who may be aware of potential procedural or practical problems. (Stakeholder and risk analyses were discussed in more detail in Chapter 2.)

In many situations the research is straightforward and there is an obvious methodology to follow. However, when the research question is complex and there are few precedents on how best to proceed it may be helpful to promote a dialogue with potential suppliers. This can often help in clarifying the definition of the problem and ensure that the research is feasible. The consultation may highlight other risks or particular issues, such as availability of the data or timescales that may need to be addressed. Collaboration will also make it more likely that good proposals will be submitted.

There are downsides in engaging with suppliers, which need to be weighed. Consultation involves more effort and will delay the project start date. One supplier must not be led to believe that they will be preferred as a result of any communication. An even-handed approach must be taken when dealing with suppliers as it would not be ethical to communicate the ideas of one supplier to others if they were to be in competition. If consultations with the research community are to take place it is advisable to arrange meetings where all potential suppliers can be present. Alternatively, one expert could be engaged as a consultant to help clarify the issues, but that person (or organisation) would then be excluded from the subsequent competition.

Being clear in one's own mind the next step is to make the specification clear to potential contractors who might undertake the work. A specification should be:

- crystal clear
- concise
- contain only essential information (background information can be appended or weblinks given to relevant sources)
- output driven.

The first three are unsurprising and need little elaboration, although they should never be overlooked. Inclusion of unnecessary information, a lengthy, ambiguous and discursive document will only lead to confusion and lack of focus on the part of those responding.

The fourth, output driven, is more controversial and requires explanation. The advice coming from procurement specialists, certainly within government and given to government social researchers, is that the specification should state *what is wanted* from the research not how the research should be done. This is sometimes difficult for social science researchers (when they are commissioning research) to accept. They often feel that their expertise should lead them to state, or at least outline, the preferred methodology. But it is not always clear at the outset what the preferred method should be, and one professional cannot be an expert in every aspect. Of course, on many occasions the method may be obvious or defined by the project itself, such as in a study requiring a household survey, but even within a prescribed methodology there may be various options that the research suppliers can contemplate.

The importance of the advice, to focus on outputs and leave the research supplier latitude to be creative over the method to be adopted, was brought home to me when I assisted an organisation to get its research programme off the ground. One question that needed answering was the extent to which young people took part in voluntary activity. Having struggled to think of the best way to conduct the research we simply invited several organisations to propose solutions and were surprised at the range of suggestions we received, many we had not thought of. It was obvious from the responses that the research organisations we approached had a great deal of expertise and experience of engaging young people in research and had well tried and tested strategies for undertaking such a study.

The social researcher commissioning the research should certainly not feel undervalued by leaving potential suppliers to propose the approach. The social researchers' skills are needed to perform the role of intelligent customer, specifying what needs to done, judging the bids and facilitating the research and collaborating with the contractors.

Essential elements of a specification of requirement

Government social researchers working with procurement colleagues in the Office of the Deputy Prime Minister developed the following template for preparing a specification of requirement. The template sets out the kind of information the potential supplier needs to know in order to prepare a bid and what specific issues the supplier needs to address in his or her bid. The template is not intended to be used prescriptively (although it represents a good model, especially for large and complex projects) but offered as guidance or a checklist of essential points to be considered.

Guidance on preparing and structuring a specification of requirement

Heading

Specification of requirement followed by the full title of the research project.

Purpose

A concise simple statement of the purpose of the research – why the information is needed.

Aims and objectives

A clear statement of the broad objective of the research, that is, a statement of what the research is required to achieve.

Issues and scope

A list of the issues that the proposal must address and any information regarding the scope of the research (as defined by geographical coverage, sample size, type of research subjects) to assist tenderers understand the range and limits of the research project. This should also identify perceived risks to the project.

Detailed requirements

In many cases it may be necessary to expand on the statement of the broad objective of the research by breaking it down into a list of more detailed objectives; that is, what is required from the research. Some of these may be presented as mandatory requirements that must be covered by the research; others may be presented as a list of desirable requirements for the tenderer to consider covering in their proposal and commenting on. Tenderers may be invited to consider other relevant objectives of the research project in their proposal that may provide added value.

Programme of work

The tenderer should be invited to propose how they will meet these requirements – a statement of the method – in the form of a programme of work. It is also recommended that they also be asked to identify any anticipated risks/difficulties/constraints that may have to be overcome in achieving the programme of work, including their proposed solutions for overcoming them.

Outputs

These are the deliverables expected from the research; normally interim, draft and final reports but also include presentations and organising seminars and, perhaps, datasets. The tenderer should be asked to identify the most effective means for ensuring that the results of the work are taken up and applied in practice, that is, impact and exploitation should be mapped out in the form of a dissemination strategy.

Performance and quality

The levels of performance and quality of inputs required to carry out the work should be described plus a description of the quality of the required outputs. If you require the tenderers to demonstrate their internal quality system control procedures, it is a good idea to ask them to submit a quality plan with their proposal.

Project plan

Tenderers should be invited to submit a project plan in support of their programme of work. This should be accompanied by a breakdown of the resource in person days allocated to each task (a resource plan).

Project team

This should describe the skills, expertise and qualifications expected of staff employed on the work. Tenderers should be requested to state who will undertake the work together with an assessment of their suitability for the work. They should also be invited to state whether subcontractors will be engaged and how the work will be managed.

Management

This should describe how the contract would be managed by the commissioning body, who would normally nominate an officer to oversee the contract and be the point of contact. If there is to be a steering group, say how often it will meet, preferably linked to key milestone deliverables in the project plan and give the arrangements for reporting progress by the contractor during the course of the project so that the contractor can build these into their quality plan.

Duration

Set a realistic date for delivering interim and final outputs, which may be negotiable dependent on the tender's proposed programme of work. If there is no scope for extending the deadlines then this should be clearly stated.

Evaluation criteria

Explain on what basis the tenders will be evaluated. This may be a simple statement such as best value for money or the list of criteria that will be used for evaluation purposes.

Annex

Background note

It is good practice to provide a comprehensive background note, which should convey information essential to the formulation of effective tenders to which knowledgeable tenderers would not normally have access.

Additional information

Other information will be needed from tenderers and tenderers will need to be informed of the timetable for the various stages of the tendering process. [*This additional information could be included within the specification but some funders address these issues in the covering letter or in other documents (my addition).*]

Price schedule

The tenderer should be informed of what information is required from them on the price of the contract, usually the total cost and how that is comprised, staff costs (daily rates or pay scales), overheads, travel and subsistence and other equipment or related costs.

Tenderers also need to be told on what date their proposals need to be submitted and in what form and how many copies. They should also be given the date that they may be required for interview (if interviews are anticipated).

[*Many government departments, in particular, also send tenderers a copy of the department's standard contract and terms and conditions so that tenderers have full prior knowledge of the contractual obligations that they will be entering into (my addition).*]

Two examples of SoRs are reproduced at the end of this chapter. They are contrasting in the level of detail given and the extent to which they prescribe the research that is to be carried out. Between them they serve to illustrate that SoRs need not all be one and the same. The only necessity is that they clearly convey what is wanted and provide enough information to enable a supplier to prepare a good proposal.

Project budget

Perhaps the most contested issue in commissioning social research is whether funders should reveal to prospective competitors the budget they have allocated for the project. Procurement rules in most central government departments preclude divulging information on budget. The justification being that if bidders knew the budget they would all cost their proposals at just under that figure. How then, procurement specialists argue, would the commissioner ever know if they could have got the work done at a lower price?

Potential contractors' counterargument is that if they are not given details of the budget how do they know what scale of project to propose? Any research project can vary in size or cost depending on whether a small number of research subjects or a large number participate, whether a few or many case studies are undertaken or whether the participant observation lasts for a short period or a long period. Furthermore, suppliers argue, if the commissioning body is judging tenders on value for money not price (as they claim to be), even if all tenders come in at a similar price, some will be offering more for that price, or the same work but to a higher quality. The commissioner will thus have choices (and perhaps more choice) if several are not ruled out immediately on cost grounds. Finally, suppliers point out that other funders, including some government departments (although not the central London 'Whitehall' departments) have no difficulty in stating the budget.

If the budget is not stated at the outset, the specification should make clear the intended scale of the work so that suppliers can make a judgement about the likely cost. The SRA guidance endorses this approach and stops short of recommending that the budget be stated.

Unfortunately the issue is usually couched in black and white terms: one should never state the budget or one should always give it. My own view is that the rules should not be so rigidly formulated and there should be more flexibility. There are circumstances where it is appropriate not to reveal the budget and on other occasions where it would be helpful. Surveys are an example of where it may not be helpful to reveal the budget. Survey companies wish to know the parameters of the survey, sample size, desired response rate, the length of the questionnaire, face-to-face or telephone interview, etc. From this information they can readily cost the survey. Being given the budget does not necessarily help; do they propose a larger sample and a shorter question-naire or some other combination?

On the other hand, stating the budget may be beneficial. In situations where research is needed but it is genuinely not known how much it would cost (perhaps there are no clear precedents on how to proceed) it may be better to reveal what budget is available and see what is offered for that price. In certain situations it may actually be anti-competitive not to reveal the budget. I know of one instance where a researcher felt that she had had a head start in a compe-tition to repeat a project she had done before because she knew how much the project had costed last time – information denied to her competitors.

Other funders, such as small charities or local authorities, may have a limited budget for the research and no prospect of obtaining additional money. In such situations it may be best to state what the budget is in order that bidders can decide whether it is possible to do the work within the prescribed budget. In my experience it is not uncommon for such bodies to reveal their budget and

I have never known it work to their disadvantage (quite the reverse as suppliers agree the fixed price and invariably finish up doing more).

Running a competition

A competition can be made open to all or restricted to a few pre-selected research suppliers. Much health research sponsored by the Department of Health is commissioned via an *open competition*. An announcement is placed in the public domain, possibly an advertisement in the British Medical Journal, and any researcher may submit a proposal for consideration. The advantage of open competition is just that. All suppliers can enter the competition, which is seen to be fair. The disadvantage is that a very large number of suppliers might bid, incurring a large cost for suppliers collectively and a large cost for the commissioning body, which then has to sift them. The opposite can also occur in that it is not unknown for no supplier to bid. There are also some indications that by being too inclusive some suppliers are put off by the low prospects of winning the contract.

Other major government departments, and most other funders, operate what they call a *selective tendering* system. This itself may be a two-stage process in that a large number of organisations are contacted initially to see if they would like to express an interest in undertaking the research. Many government departments publish a research programme early in the financial year listing the projects that they will be commissioning throughout the year and inviting researchers to express interest at that stage. Recording an expression of interest invariably entails completing a two-page form briefly stating why the organisation is qualified to undertake the work and, in the broadest terms, stating how the researchers would carry out the work. From these initial expressions, a subset will be invited to prepare full proposals for detailed consideration. The advantage of a two-stage process is that the competition can be opened up to many suppliers but only those selected for the second stage are required to invest considerable time preparing a full proposal. The disadvantage is that the protracted procedures add time to the period before the supplier is contracted and the research can begin.

Whom to invite?

How many organisations should be invited to compete? If it is decided to adopt the two-stage process it is advisable to call for expressions of interest from a wide selection of organisations. How many should be selected to prepare full proposals should depend on the response to the expression of interest stage, indicating the availability of suitable suppliers (if that prior stage was held), and on the size and complexity of the project. It is generally thought to be a broad procurement rule to have at least three suppliers bidding. However, not all invitees will bid so it is common to issue invitations to five or six for most medium-sized projects, and more for very large projects. To minimise the number who will not respond, it is helpful to phone the selected potential suppliers to make sure that they are still, or would be, interested in bidding at that time. If some are not, others can be substituted before invitations are sent out. The practice also alerts those who are interested that time will need to be set aside to prepare a proposal.

The type of organisation to invite will largely depend on the nature of the work. The most obvious example is that if a large national survey is required, survey companies specialising in that type of research will be invited. For most studies, however, the decision on whom to invite is not always so clear-cut. Invariably, to undertake a research project a mixture of knowledge of the substantive area and methodological research skills will be required. If it is not clear whom to invite, the two-stage process described above could be a way forward in order to identify potential contractors and to narrow down the options. Be prepared to take risks. Staying with the familiar, tried and tested suppliers will ensure a good product but may minimise innovation. It is considered to be good practice to invite one supplier who has not worked for the commissioning body before. This practice introduces an element of new blood and encourages new organisations into the market. Importantly, the new supplier may offer an approach which the established suppliers may not have considered.

Commissioning procedures

Having decided which suppliers to invite, it is imperative to treat all in an equal and fair manner (the proverbial 'level playing field'). The specification of requirement and supporting documentation should be sent to all invitees at the same time from the same location in the same way. It is felt to be good practice not to reveal who else has been invited so that all are competing blind. However, I have experienced occasions where a list of all invitees has been included within the documentation. This may be appropriate where the research is especially complex and the commissioner may wish suppliers to team up in consortiums in order that they may better provide the range of skills that will be required. But, if this procedure is adopted, everyone must be treated in the same way – all are blind or all are aware of the other bidders.

All suppliers should be given the same time to respond; that is, a time and date by which proposals are to be submitted should be clearly indicated in the covering letter. A suitable period should be allowed, especially if suppliers need to team up with others or consult amongst themselves in developing a method and plan for the work. Three weeks is considered to be the absolute minimum but five is regarded as preferable. But three working weeks – I was once invited to bid on 16 December and my response had to be submitted by 6 January!

Once the invitations have been sent out, issues arise over whether the commissioner should have contact with the potential suppliers during the period that they have been given to prepare their proposal. Again the principle to be followed is to treat everyone even-handedly. It may be sensible to contact all invitees after a week to check if they will be submitting a proposal. Some government departments now formally request invited suppliers to complete and return a form part way into the period stating whether or not they will be bidding. This provides further indication of how many (and who) will be bidding and provides a further opportunity to take remedial action if an insufficient number are intending to submit proposals. Of course, any new potential suppliers brought into the competition at this stage have to be given the same time to prepare a proposal as the original invitees. This may necessitate keeping the original bids unopened and secure (they should not be given longer) until the second batch arrives.

It is likely that some invitees will contact the commissioner during this period. They may have queries about the specification, which require further clarification. If so these should be answered – it is in everyone's interest to be clear about what is wanted. However, any answers given to one should be circulated anonymously to all the others. The more difficult judgements occur when the research supplier sounds the commissioner out on bright ideas they may have had about how to carry out the work. The issue here is whether what they are proposing constitutes their intellectual property, something that they exclusively have developed, or whether it is something that any researcher could have thought of? If the former then it should not be passed to others. However, my experience is that the pretext is invariably contrived in order that the supplier can make themselves known to the commissioner. My response would most likely be to suggest that they put the bright idea in the proposal, perhaps as an alternative approach to be considered.

On some occasions the commissioner may want to initiate a meeting with all invitees jointly to resolve or clarify particular issues. I once bid for research, which involved secondary analysis of a complex administrative dataset. As the potential contractors needed to have a clear understanding of the coverage and layout of the data and how it would need to be accessed, the commissioner held a meeting to explain the technicalities – a matter that was too complex to describe in a background note accompanying the specification. However, one needs to be clear about the purpose of such a meeting and how it is to be run. A meeting should only be held for the purpose of the commissioner conveying essential information that will aid the competition, not as a method of seeking ideas from potential contractors. If the views of the wider research community were needed, that input should have been obtained before the SoR was sent out. (In any case feedback won't be forthcoming at such meetings as most will attend to observe with whom they are in competition and they certainly will not be sharing their good ideas in a public gathering.)

At the end of the period a standardised procedure should be in place to receive and register submitted proposals. It is considered good practice to keep them sealed until a pre-specified time and date when they are all opened in the presence of more than one nominated person – one to register, the other to witness the procedure. The submitted proposals can then be distributed to all who will be required to evaluate them. What to do with those that arrive late? Most funders would not consider late arrivals unless there is evidence that steps were taken to submit the proposal on time and there was evidence to show that the delay was due to reasons outside the supplier's control. For example, if the supplier could verify that the proposal was posted on time from a receipt of postage or the postmark on the envelope.

Those tasked with evaluating the tenders should do this, where possible, independently. A meeting should then be arranged where a collective decision can be taken. Often a clear winner does not emerge at this stage, rather one will be seen as the preferred supplier with another close behind in second place. Or two will be considered equally good but for different reasons. Either way there will be aspects of each proposal that need to be discussed or clarified with the proposers. The period from negotiation to contract is dealt with in Chapter 5. After negotiations have taken place, a supplier will be chosen and a contract entered into.

All unsuccessful applicants should be informed of the decision at the same time, and if it is clear that they will not be considered further, notification should not be delayed while negotiations are continuing with those who may be successful. It is advisable not to give lengthy and protracted reasons for the decision in writing but to offer oral feedback should the research supplier wish. Most will want feedback and giving feedback can be a daunting task for the representative of the commissioning body to perform. But my experience (from both giving feedback and from receiving it) is that it is not confrontational; simply that having put in a lot of effort into preparing a proposal it is always helpful to receive comments. Unsuccessful bidders are pleased to hear of some good features of their proposal and can usually recognise and accept the reasons for failure, which may well have been outside their control in any case. Whatever the reason, lessons can be learnt for the future.

Throughout the competition it is imperative to document procedures. Organisations may require an audit trail to be kept. But even if not, it is often difficult to remember retrospectively what was said and how certain decisions were arrived at and on what basis.

European Union Procurement Rules

The EU Procurement Rules seek to implement uniform, open and fair competition across member states regarding procurement by public bodies. Public bodies are taken to be government departments, quangos and NDPBs and local authorities and even public utilities. Other bodies and organisations are thus excluded from the requirements imposed by the Rules. Even for public bodies the Rules apply only when the procurement is expected to be over a threshold price. For social research this is currently 200,000 euros or about £130,000. Public bodies should not deliberately underestimate the probable value of the contract or break up the work into component parts to circumvent the Rules. If the project does have to comply with the Rules, an advert inviting tenders has to be placed in the Official Journal of the European Union (OJ) enabling any organisation within the member states an opportunity to bid.

In practice, much social research commissioned by public bodies is exempt from the rules, regardless of the value of the project. However, the situation can change and anyone uncertain of their position should seek specialist procurement advice. Further information can be found on the website of The Office of Government Commerce www.ogc.gov.uk.

SPECIFICATION OF REQUIREMENT: EXAMPLE 1

Review of development of policy and costs of housing related support since 1997

Purpose

The purpose is to carry out a review of what has been happening in the 'real world' of housing-related support since 1997 (when the Divisional Court ruled that Housing Benefit should meet service charges for personal support only in limited circumstances) to inform a central strategy for Supporting People in the long term. The study will focus in particular on the Transitional Housing Benefit Scheme (THBS) between 2000 and 2003, it is not intended to cover other funding streams in any detail. The aim is not to carry out an audit but to look for the broader picture and gather more information to supplement and improve what is already available. This will require some reference to previous years in order to understand the background. This project is required urgently.

Objectives

To carry out a review of the development of housing-related support policy in England and Wales, in particular the Transitional Housing Benefit Scheme between 2000 and 2003, and to produce a report that addresses the following issues:

- To explain the patterns of Housing Benefit expenditure for general counselling and support in the period, looking for a broad-brush picture.
- How were the original and subsequent estimates made, what did they cover and how good was the evidence base, looking for a broad-brush picture?
- What factors influence demand? To what extent could those factors have been foreseen?

continued

- How important was the interaction between community care policy and housing related support policy?
- What was the role of the 'market' suppliers and providers of supported housing (RSLs, voluntary and private sector organisations) post community care? What role did these organisations play in growing the market that they had a significant interest in? During the period of the scheme, were there unintended incentive effects to provide new or additional services (bearing in mind that maximising the pot and bringing in new provision were declared aims of the Supporting People programme)?
- Has the creation of a Supporting People budget, through the use of THBS, had any impact on social services budgets? To what extent has there been cost shifting, e.g. from social services to Supporting People budgets, through the use of Transitional Housing Benefit? And what has been the impact on the Social Service budgets locally as a result of this?
- To what extent did Government policies to promote independence (e.g. Valuing People, rough sleeping, care leavers and frail elderly) interact with Supporting People policies in ways that had not been foreseen and what were the consequences?
- To what extent was it inevitable that Transitional Housing Benefit should have paid for care, rather than housing-related support? How well was this risk foreseen and how well was the risk managed?
- How important was the growth of floating support to people in their own homes in general needs housing, and how well was its importance recognised in the Transitional Housing Benefit scheme?
- To what extent did rent restructuring provide an incentive for housing associations to lower their rents by allocating more costs to support and what was the impact of this?
- How will any future changes to schemes eligible for Supporting People impact on the programmes of other government departments and what are the best ways to manage this in the run-up to the Spending Review 2004?

Scope

- Outcomes for service users are out of scope for this study, as this is being dealt with through another research programme.
- The project will cover England and Wales initially, with the option to extend the study to cover Scotland at a later stage. If that option is pursued then an additional question for the objectives will be: what was the significance of the much later process of

de-institutionalisation in Scotland, which embraced community care after, and on a longer time scale, than England and Wales?

Outputs

Written monthly progress reports will be required. A draft report for comments, a presentation of results, a four-page summary and a final report are required. Outlines will be agreed in advance with ODPM. The report should be not longer than 50 pages of A4 text plus annexes and should be written in plain language. The report is intended for publication.

Management

ODPM will appoint a Project Manager. The contractor will be required to appoint a Project Manager who will be regarded as fully accountable for delivery of the project against the contract.

There will be an advisory group consisting of representatives of: ODPM, HO, DWP, DoH, HMT, Scottish Executive and Welsh Assembly. It is envisaged that this will meet twice, at the outset to agree the approach, and prior to the draft report, to discuss the presentation of emerging findings.

Duration

This project is required urgently, work should begin by mid-June 2003 and a draft is required by the end of September 2003.

Programme of work, project plan and quality

The tender should propose a programme of work that meets the requirement and the timetable and explain how they will achieve high quality standards. The tender should identify any anticipated difficulties and constraints, together with solutions for overcoming them. The project plan should show how the work will be sequenced and be accompanied by a resource profile showing the person days allocated to each task.

Tenders should demonstrate a full understanding of the requirement and propose appropriate and innovative methods. ODPM anticipates that these will include the following methods and is also open to other approaches that will contribute to meeting the requirement:

* desk review of published and unpublished material, focusing especially on the financial estimates produced at each stage;

continued

- interviews with 25–35 key informants to be nominated by ODPM in consultation with other Departments. These will include civil servants, researchers, representatives of supported housing providers and the National Housing Federation;
- review of information and views posted on the K web discussion forum by local authorities and others.

Project team

The project requires a multi-disciplinary team with knowledge and skills in the following areas.

- Supporting People and Housing Benefit policy
- economic analysis skills
- social research skills
- synthesising and reporting complex issues in plain language.

Evaluation criteria

Best value for money taking into account:

- quality of the proposal
- proven expertise
- track record of delivery to time and budget
- cost.

Background note

DWP has published a number of relevant reports:

Research Report Number 93: 'Housing Benefit and Supported Accommodation' by Andreas Cebulla et al.

This report presents estimates of Housing Benefit claimants in Britain who were in supported accommodation in 1996/97 and of the amount of Housing Benefit spent on support services considered ineligible for Housing Benefit at that time.

In-House Report Number 73: 'Implementing the Transitional Benefit Scheme' by Kim Shrapnell and Kirby Swales, December 2000

This report presents the results of research to identify local authorities' progress in implementing the Transitional Housing Benefit Scheme

(THBS). The main aims were to find out how local authorities were progressing in identifying customers in supported accommodation, contacting providers, and reviewing claims. The research was based on a self-completion postal questionnaire that was sent to and returned by almost 400 authorities in summer 2000. This survey was conducted in-house by the DSS's Social Research Branch.

In-House Report Number 86: 'The Transitional Housing Benefits Scheme: a Three Way Process' by Roy Sainsbury and Christine Oldman, October 2001

This report presents the findings of research commissioned by DWP and DTLR into the implementation of the Transitional Housing Benefit Scheme. Six case studies carried out in early 2001 and four workshops for local authorities were hosted by DETR and DSS in April and May 2001. The case studies comprised in-depth interviews with the key stakeholders in each local authority area, including Housing Benefit managers, staff directly involved with implementing THBS, Supporting People lead officers, staff in housing and social services departments, and providers of supported accommodation. A small number of interviews with staff of Benefits Agency offices were also carried out. The workshops were attended by Housing Benefit and Supporting People staff from approximately 160 local authorities.

THBS related question modules were included in waves 3 and 6 of the DWP Omnibus Survey, which is available on the DWP website. [*There then followed details of where to find the data on the web – those details have been omitted here.*]

SPECIFICATION OF REQUIREMENT: EXAMPLE 2

'GIFTAID IN WALES' present usage and awareness of Welsh charities of Gift Aid

GIVING CAMPAIGN RESEARCH PROJECT BRIEF

Background

The Giving Campaign (TGC) aims to encourage a culture of giving in the UK and to increase the number of donors and the amount of donations. The Campaign is committed to undertaking high quality

continued

research. As well as informing the Campaign's own activities, this research is published where it is useful to others. Further information is available on the Campaign website, www.givingcampaign.org.uk.

Purpose and objectives of research project

The purpose of the present project is to ascertain:

- how many charities registered in Wales know about Gift Aid
- how many have registered with the Inland Revenue for Gift Aid
- amongst those that have registered, how much have they been able to reclaim through Gift Aid.

The objective is to produce a baseline of information to provide a starting point for the work of the TGC in Wales.

Proposed approach

The Wales Council for Voluntary Action (WCVA) has a database with the details of over 25,000 voluntary organisations active in Wales. Of these it estimates that there are around 8,000 registered charities that fall within their definition of the voluntary sector. Some of this group are small benevolent charities, which are not attracting donated income. The remaining cohort that the TGC wishes to sample, number around 5,000 charities. The TGC will supply contact details for the charities we want to be contacted.

We invite the agency to propose:

- the most effective method of contacting the relevant organisations
- to suggest what levels of response rate could be achieved within the proposed timeframe
- the questions that will need to be asked to achieve the purpose and objectives of the proposed research.

Timetable

The Campaign is being launched in Wales on Wednesday the 5th of March 2003. We will require an interim report on the findings being obtained from the research for the launch, with a final report completed by the end of March 2003.

Roles of the TGC and the agency

The Giving Campaign will oversee the project, provide the contact details and publish the results.

The role of the agency will be to produce a detailed project plan; to devise interview content and schedules; and to produce a database of the charities contacted and a final report, for publication by the Campaign. The Giving Campaign will expect to be given an opportunity to review in draft the project and interview plans and the report of findings.

Written proposals are sought *by Friday 24 January 2003*. These should include a clear explanation of how the interviews would be structured so as to provide insights in the relevant areas, a timetable for carrying out the project, and a budget for the costs of the work. Short listed bidders will be invited to present their proposals to members of The Giving Campaign Research Group on the morning of *Wednesday 30 January 2003* in Cardiff. The selected agency will be the one which persuades us they will deliver results in a cost effective, efficient, technically robust and creative way, within the time constraints set out above.

The Giving Campaign

4 Applying for research funding

It can be easily overlooked, but much social research (for example, theoretical research, secondary analysis of data, some qualitative research) is not dependent on financial support but can be undertaken with few resources other than the investigator's own time. A good deal of academic research is of this kind and in the course of a long research career it is refreshing and intellectually stimulating to be able to have periods where one can set and work to one's own agenda without the pressures of competing for money. Nevertheless, these moments are becoming rare as institutional pressures mount to win financial support for research, and most empirical research which requires extensive data collection will need to be resourced.

This chapter briefly describes opportunities for obtaining funds for social research before going on to offer guidance on how to prepare a research proposal.

Modes of research funding

At the extremes there are two main modes of funding social research: responsive and prescriptive, although, increasingly, much research is funded by a mode which falls somewhere in-between.

Responsive mode

This method of funding research is characteristic of the research councils and charities in that the research community initiates ideas for research, prepares proposals and submits them to the funding body for consideration. The funding body will have a procedure in place to send proposals to peer reviewers and others who may be interested in the research and to collate the comments and judgements made. In light of the peer reviews, a panel will consider all the applications received, prioritise them and award grants to those that come sufficiently high in the rank order.

The significant features of this form of funding is that the researcher decides what is worth doing and how it might be done. In the process of reviewing applications, peer reviewers or the panel arbitrating on the proposals may feel the research is not important or not adequately scientifically specified and the proposal may be unsuccessful for that reason. However, if it is judged to be worthy and of sufficient priority, and secures funding, the researcher is left to pursue the research as proposed. The only requirement will be to submit a report at the end of the award. On occasions the funding body may impose conditions but these are more to do with the logistics (ensuring that the data is available, access will be granted, etc.) or details of finance. The funding body will not enter into lengthy discussions to modify the proposal or tell the researcher how it might be differently undertaken.

Prescriptive mode

Prescriptive mode (also known as directive mode) is the method of funding operated by government departments in particular (although virtually all funders will let some contracts this way). Through some deliberation over policy or practice the government department will have identified an issue that they wish to address through research and will be looking for an organisation to undertake the research. Invariably they will prepare a specification of their requirement and invite a number of research suppliers to be involved in a competitive process to bid to do the work.

The important characteristics of this form of funding are that the funder is the customer for the research and sets the requirements and the parameters of the research. The researcher has to agree to meet that requirement and work within those constraints. Because the customer has a vision of what is required, there is likely to be a period of negotiation between the customer and the supplier before agreement is reached and a contract signed. Furthermore, the customer is likely to take an active interest in the project during its life cycle and be involved in discussions about any changes to the project that might be needed.

Hybrid: part prescriptive part responsive

The above presented the two extremes, but increasingly more research is being funded through a mixture of prescriptive and responsive modes. Here the funding body will identify particular themes that it wishes research to address. A dedicated amount of money is set aside to fund that theme (often referred to as a programme) and the research community is invited to come up with proposals for research that falls within the remit of the programme. The EU has always funded research in this way through its Framework Programme. The ESRC has in the past set up various programmes; recent examples include: Democracy and Participation, Growing Older, E-society and Future of Work. Each programme will, typically, exist for three to four years, have a dedicated budget of between £3 to 4 million, and sponsor twenty individual projects. Charities can only fund research that falls within their charitable purposes, so to that extent they have always been prescriptive. Within their remit, further research priorities are set. For example, the Joseph Rowntree Foundation have established committees to take forward priority themes, including Housing and Neighbourhoods, Poverty and Disadvantage, Drugs and Alcohol, Parenting. Each committee periodically issues 'calls for proposals' to address particular issues within those priority themes.

The advantages of programmes are that they can prioritise particularly important or neglected topics for research and concentrate effort on it for a fixed period of time by funding a range of related projects. Funders also take the view that the whole is greater than the sum of the parts. Synergies can be formed bringing researchers together and value added through the interchange of ideas and experiences. The public impact of a programme can be coordinated and the funder will often appoint a Programme Director who will take a more direct interest in the projects throughout the period of the programme. A Steering Committee or an Advisory Committee may also be appointed. The researchers working on the individual projects may be obliged to participate in programme-wide activities such as programme workshops and programme dissemination strategies.

Funders of social research

The world wide web has considerably simplified the task of obtaining details of current opportunities for research funding. Most major commissioners and funders of social research have well-developed websites which announce calls for proposals, state their current thematic priorities, their criteria of eligibility, guidance for applicants and even provide online application forms. It is not necessary to provide a detailed description for each funding body here (and any details provided might soon be out-of-date so would require verifying at source). What is given is an overview and directions to obtain further information.

As mentioned in Chapter 1, the research councils, the EU and charities are the main 'responsive mode' funders of social research for those researchers seeking support for research they have initiated themselves. The only constraint is that the project may have to fall within a theme that has been prioritised, or in the case of charities, within their area of interest or charitable aims. Government departments and other public bodies set the agenda and invite research suppliers to undertake the work.

The Research Councils

Of the eight UK Research Councils, the Economic and Social Research Council (www.esrc.ac.uk) is entirely dedicated to social science research and the main funder, spending around £68 million per annum on social research. (This figure does not include the £26 million spent on postgraduate training.) A proportion of the money (£13 million) is set aside for core support for specific research centres (such as, the Centre for Economic Performance (CEP), the

Transport Studies Unit (TSU) and the Centre for Economic Aspects of Genomics (CESAGen)) and a proportion (£6 million) to support method-ological developments and the infrastructure of social research (such as the Economic and Social Data Service). This tranche of funding is administered by the Research Resources Board. Of the remainder, £15 million is allocated to support specific research programmes (such as, Future Governance, Evaluation of Business Knowledge) and the largest amount, £16.5 million, to fund indi-vidual grant applications initiated by social researchers themselves. (The remaining £16 million is spent on research fellowships (see below), other research infrastructure and equipment, other research methods and teaching and learning initiatives.)

Only academics working in higher education institutions and ESRC approved (mainly not-for-profit) independent social research centres are eligible for ESRC funding (or funding from any research council). Opportunities to bid for programme funding only arise at the inception of the specific programme, but grant applications can be made at any time (although an appli-cation may have to wait for the next cycle of the decision-making process.) Grant applications are divided into small grants (currently those less than £40 k) and large grants (£40 k to £750 k – the maximum that the ESRC will grant). Small grants are subject to a 'light touch', being reviewed by only two people, permitting decisions to be made relatively quickly on whether or not to fund the research. Large grants, on the other hand, are more extensively reviewed and prioritised by the Research Grants Board alongside other large grants.

The ESRC maintains a database of research it has funded or is currently funding (as well as providing a gateway to other online resources) which can be searched to identify previous or ongoing similar research. The database can be accessed at www.esrc.ac.uk/ESRCInfoCentre/research.

Although the ESRC is the main sponsor, other research councils offer social scientists opportunities for support. The subject area of the Arts and Humanities Research Council (AHRC) (www.ahrc.ac.uk) overlaps considerably with ESRC's areas of interest, so much so that the two research councils have issued a joint statement on Subject Coverage (see AHRB website for details). Two examples serve to delineate their respective responsibilities. History: the AHRB is the main sponsor of historical research but the ESRC will consider applications addressing aspects of social and economic history. Law: the AHRB funds research on the content or procedures of law whereas the ESRC funds socio-legal studies, which reflect a focus on the socio-economic impact of the law and the legal system. Having read the guidance, if a social researcher is still not clear which council to submit the application to, a quick telephone call to either council should resolve the matter.

The Medical Research Council (MRC) (www.mrc.ac.uk) funds research in the area it defines as 'People and Population Studies', that is, research on the effect of social and economic factors on health, including such social behaviours as smoking, drinking and drug use. (Obviously an application to the MRC would be considerably strengthened if the social researcher applies jointly with a medical researcher.)

While not a research council (and primarily funding science, engineering and technological (SET) research), the Royal Society (www.royalsoc.ac.uk) does fund what it describes as 'Health and Human Sciences' research. As with applications to the MRC, applications to the Royal Society have a better chance of success if they have a SET 'edge' or component or if submitted jointly with a SET scientist.

European Union

The European Union funds research in various ways but mainly through its Framework Programme. Each FP lasts for three to four years; the one in operation now is FP6, covering the period 2003–06. (FP7 is currently being formulated through consultations and discussions.) The overall budget for FP6 for the four years is 17.5 billion euros. Seven thematic areas have been identified:

1   Life sciences, genomics and biotechnology for health
2   Information society technologies
3   Nanotechnologies and nano-sciences, knowledge-based multifunctional materials and new production processes and devices
4   Aeronautics and space
5   Food quality and safety
6   Sustainable development, global change and ecosystems
7   Citizens and governance in a knowledge-based society.

It can be seen that most of the research supported is science, engineering and technology (SET), only one thematic area (the seventh) is specifically devoted to social science. Nevertheless, some limited opportunity for social research exists within the other thematic areas, often in collaboration with researchers from other disciplinary backgrounds. A Framework Programme is 'rolled out' through 'calls' issued periodically during the four-year period. Each call will invite expressions of interest or full proposals on a particular sub-topic within a thematic area. It is rare for the EU to fund single-centre applications, preferring to fund a consortium of collaborating research institutes across a range of EU member states. It is thus imperative to find 'partners' for any proposed project.

Detailed information on EU funding opportunities, including how to apply and how to find partners can be found at the Community Research and Development Information Service (CORDIS) website (http://fp6.cordis.lu/fp6/home.cfm).

In order to assist the research community to apply for EU grants, the six research councils have jointly established the UK Research Office (UKRO) based in Brussels. UKRO services are only available to subscribers but most universities have subscribed so academics will be able to access the service. The annual subscription is not cheap, at approximately £3,000 per annum for academic institutions and voluntary sector organisations. Further information is available at the UKRO website (www.ukro.ac.uk).

Charities

The main charities funding social research are the Joseph Rowntree Foundation, the Nuffield Foundation and the Leverhulme Trust, but they will only fund research on a topic that falls within their area of interest.

The Joseph Rowntree Foundation (www.jrf.org.uk) supports research on housing, social care and social policy. Within each area thematic programmes are prioritised.

The Nuffield Foundation (www.nuffieldfoundation.org) funds social research in the following areas: child protection, family law and justice, access to justice and older people and their families. However, projects of exceptional merit outside these areas will be considered.

The Leverhulme Trust (www.leverhulme.org.uk) is not restricted in the research it can support but priorities are set and change periodically.

The Carnegie Trust (www.carnegie-trust.org) is also of note as it too supports research, but only research undertaken by graduates of Scottish Universities or research based at Scottish Universities.

A multitude of other smaller trusts currently fund or have been known to fund social science research but space precludes listing them here. A good source of information is the Charities Aid Foundation (CAF) *Directory of Grant Giving Trusts*. This Directory, which is published annually in two volumes, can be found in any sizeable local authority or higher educational institution library. The vast majority of trusts listed do not fund research but other programmes and activities, so it can be a time-consuming job identifying those that do.

Research funding is also available from the National Lotteries Charities Board, also now known as the Big Lottery Fund (www.nlcb.org.uk). The Research Grant Programme dispenses £8 million per year for social and medical research in four priority areas: young people, older people, people with learning difficulties and people from black and ethnic minority groups. However, only voluntary sector organisations are eligible to *apply* for the research grants. Although universities are charities and thus legally qualified to apply they are excluded as matter of policy by NLCB. If the eligible voluntary sector organisation does not have the in-house capacity or capability to undertake the research it can enter into partnership with another research supplier (e.g. a university or research centre), but the voluntary sector organisation must take the lead in applying for funding and in managing the project.

Government departments

Most UK government departments (and certainly all the major ones) sponsor social research although the budgets for research vary considerably between them. For further information about this sector an excellent starting point is the Government Social Research website (www.gsr.gov.uk). Social researchers are employed in eighteen different departments. A brief description of the areas of work and the organisation of research in each department is given together with a link to the department's own website where further information can be obtained.

The department's own website will invariably contain a copy of the department's research programme and details of its procedures for commissioning research. A list of published research reports are available and increasingly, as more are published electronically, the reports themselves can be downloaded from the website.

As government departments operate by inviting research suppliers to bid for contracts, the issue for the new researcher is to make themselves (and their organisation) known to the department such that they might be invited to bid. Some departments, but by no means all, publish annual programmes of research detailing the projects they will be sponsoring in the coming year. If produced, that document will be at the department's website and will invite researchers to submit an 'expression of interest' by completing a short form briefly outlining the credentials and suitability of the organisation to undertake the work. When it comes to commissioning the project during the year the department will consider all those who have expressed an interest. Again, some departments, but not all, have established a formal database of known research suppliers, which can be referred to when seeking a pool of potential contractors for a project. The website may give details of how an organisation might register on that database. Failing all else a researcher seeking to become established should simply 'cold call' the Head of Research in the department to enquire what procedures the department has adopted to select research suppliers for its contracts.

The Department of Health operates differently from other government departments. In the previous chapter it was pointed out that the Department of Health funds a significant number of dedicated research centres, but much of the rest of its social research is commissioned via open tender. An announcement of the requirement is placed in the media (principally the *Guardian*, the *Health Service Journal*, the *British Medical Journal* and the *Nursing Times*) and also on the Department's website. Anyone can respond by obtaining the detailed specification of requirement and by submitting a proposal. The Department does not pre-select a shortlist of suppliers, which it invites to bid.

Although outside the scope of this book, readers may wish to be aware that the GSR website advertises vacancies for research posts within government.

Fellowships

The ESRC, the British Academy (www.britac.ac.uk), Leverhulme, Nuffield and Carnegie have set aside a proportion of their funds to finance fellowships. Rather than supporting a project the fellowship supports an individual researcher for a fixed period and schemes are available to researchers at every stage of their career. Many are directed at researchers having just completed their PhD and are looking to become established in research. However, others exist to relieve more experienced researchers from other administrative or teaching duties in order that they can devote their full attention to undertaking or completing a programme of research. There are even fellowships to support recently retired academics.

Details of current funding opportunities is the publication *Research Fortnight*, which (not surprisingly) is published every two weeks and lists all announcements or calls for proposals by the main grant-making bodies. *Research Fortnight* covers all areas of research and most of its content relates to the physical, natural and medical sciences and less to the social sciences. Furthermore, it does not provide a comprehensive list government sponsored research, which is often by invitation only and not open to all to apply. *Research Fortnight* is expensive to subscribe to, over £400 per year, but many large research institutions will have subscribed and copies will be available to researchers working in them.

Preparing a proposal

Following the distinction drawn above between responsive and prescriptive modes of funding, the researcher may have a particular research interest or a good idea for research and seeks funding. The objective here is to identify a funding body that is responsive to such research applications and then to convince that body that the proposal is worthy (more worthy than other applications it may have received) and should thereby be accorded sufficiently high priority to qualify for support.

Alternatively, a researcher may have received a specification of requirement from a commissioning body outlining a research question to be answered and have been invited to submit a bid to carry out the work. In this situation the researcher will be in direct competition with other organisations who have also been invited to bid. The objective here is to demonstrate to the commissioner that the researcher has the credentials and a plan to undertake the work well, and better than the other bidders, and, furthermore, that his or her proposal offers the best value for money.

Whether applying for a grant to support your research idea or responding to an invitation to tender, it is first important to read carefully (and understand fully) all instructions issued by the funding or commissioning body. To apply, the applicant must first be eligible, that is, a bona fide organisation under the remit of the funding body, and the subject of the research must fall within the topic areas that the funding body can support. Each funding body will operate within certain boundaries and set out conditions or restrictions. These might include:

- the size of the grant
- the duration of the project
- the constituent elements for which financial support is given
- the layout of the application
- the appropriate form to be used
- the word length of the application
- the date by which the application should be submitted.

It is surprising how often one hears sponsors and commissioners of research complain that applicants did not follow basic rules when preparing or submitting an application. Errors on the form do not always rule out an application but it can often be detrimental as it may raise concerns about an applicant's competence. In a climate where there are many good applications from which to choose, provoking any adverse reaction is to be avoided.

On what basis will an application be judged?

Insight into how an application will be judged can be instructive when preparing a proposal. Applications to the ESRC are sent for peer review as well as being assessed by members of the relevant Research Grants or Programme Board who are experts in their chosen field. The applications are marked according to a scale, which varies depending on whether it is a small grant or a large grant and whether it is to be judged by an external academic referee, internal Board Assessor/Member or whether by a representative of the user community. The details are confusing and not relevant as all projects in competition with each other are marked on the same scale. What are important are the four key criteria that reviewers and assessors are requested to take into account. They are:

1   originality: potential contribution to knowledge
2   research design and methods
3   value for money
4   communication strategy and planned output.

As a member of a team recently tasked to examine the ESRC procedures for granting awards, and in particular to consider why some social science disciplines appear to be more successful than others, it was clear that reviewers did deliberate over all four criteria. Around 300 applications were examined together with the marks and comments of reviewers. In addition, thirty reviewers were interviewed. Reviewers did not always feel themselves to be competent at judging 'communication strategy and planned output' although they were keen to see that a strategy had been clearly formulated. 'Value for money' posed problems too, although some projects fell because it was clear that a large amount of money was requested even though very little fieldwork was to be carried out. Thus criteria 3 and 4 could have a large negative effect but applied to few applications.

It was clear that reviewers felt most competent to judge the theoretical and methodological aspects of an application encompassed in the first two criteria. Assessment of 'research design and methods' was a technical and professional judgement of whether the proposed method was feasible, doable and was appropriate and robust enough to uncover the information and test the hypothesis. Once satisfied that the application scored well on the other three criteria, 'originality: potential contribution to knowledge' seemed paramount. Key for reviewers was that the boundaries of knowledge would (or at least potentially could) be pushed forward by the research, that knowledge would advance as a result of the project. Several said that when considering a project they ask the question 'so what'? That is, will scientific knowledge be the poorer for not funding the project? If the answer is no, the application is effectively doomed.

An application submitted to a government department following an invitation to tender will be assessed by the Evaluation Panel assembled for that project. The Panel most likely will comprise a member of the department's social research group, another professional analyst (for example, a statistician or economist), the main policy customer (who will have requested the project and be extremely knowledgeable about the context for the research) and, perhaps, a practitioner (who will bring insights regarding the setting of the research and the subjects of the research).

The criteria they will apply will have been set out in the specification of requirement (discussed in Chapter 3). Universal criteria most commonly applied include:

- understanding of the assignment/development of the research brief
- feasibility and efficiency of the design/methodology/outputs proposed
- relevant experience of the researchers/organisation (and subcontractors where relevant)/track record
- project management/suitability of working arrangements
- suitability of timetable and ability to meet it
- cost and value for money
- quality assurance control mechanisms.

Other criteria may be added depending on the specific characteristics of the research, for example, if the research addresses particularly sensitive issues or engages particular subject groups such as children, the elderly, those with learning difficulties. In these situations the government department may place more emphasis on ethical issues, previous skills and experience or plans to overcome potential difficulties.

Specific topics to be addressed when preparing a proposal

Whether applying for a grant or responding to an invitation to tender I offer a checklist of specific topics that need to be considered. Of course, not all will feature in every proposal and the emphasis will change according to the requirements of the particular situation. Nevertheless all should be thought through if only to be dismissed. And, to re-emphasise, this checklist should be considered alongside the specific instructions originating from the commissioning or funding body.

Makes the case for research/understands the issues

If applying for a grant to support research you have initiated you have obviously got to convince the review panel that the topic needs researching and should receive priority. The proposal has to communicate the theoretical and scientific knowledge which will stem from the research and why it is important and timely to undertake the research now. Set out how the frontiers of knowledge will be advanced or enhancements to practice will be achieved as a result of the project. Who will benefit from the research and how will they benefit? Above all, state clearly and intelligibly the aims and objectives for the project. It is also essential to convey your and the team's interest, enthusiasm and commitment for the research.

If responding to an invitation to tender the approach is obviously different. The commissioner has stated that they want the research undertaken, so the researcher has to show that he or she fully understands the issues they want addressing. In their guidance, government departments state that they are looking for awareness of the context of the research and thought about the research aims. Do not merely reiterate what is in the specification of requirement but attempt to show how the understanding you bring to the topic will generate further insights and add value in developing the aims of the research.

Builds on previous relevant research/has relevant knowledge

In responsive mode the researcher will need to demonstrate that the research issue has been properly formulated and relates to current scientific and theoretical debates and builds on previous relevant research. A significant proportion of the proposal will hence be devoted to critiquing existing theoretical discourse and justifying a theoretical framework for the research. It is also expected to review previous literature in some depth in order to identify gaps in knowledge and to set the context for the study. At the barest minimum the proposal needs to confirm that the research or similar research has not been done before (unless the aim is to replicate previous research).

When responding to an invitation to tender, the emphasis will be different. Much of the literature may be referenced in the specification of requirement and the commissioner will be unlikely to be seeking developments in theory from the research. In such cases it may actually be a disadvantage to devote undue attention to theory or previous literature as the review panel may interpret this as an indication that the proposer has an 'academic' agenda that is more important to them than meeting the commissioner's objectives. Nevertheless, if literature exists that may have been overlooked or which specifically develops the research aims it should be cited and its significance highlighted. Similarly, theoretical perspectives that are important to the research aims should not be ignored. Regardless of how literature and theory are presented the researcher needs to demonstrate that he or she has the relevant knowledge that enables them to understand the nuances of the issues to be addressed and can utilise that knowledge to the benefit of the project.

Stakeholder analysis

Have all the stakeholders been identified and do any need to be contacted either to lend support to the project (and thereby strengthen its chances of success) or to facilitate access to data or research subjects? The proposal will need to state that stakeholders have agreed to cooperate with the research.

A specification of requirement will probably identify stakeholders but even here it will be important to clarify in the proposal how the stakeholders will be approached and engaged in the research.

Risk assessment

Consider all risks. What is problematic, what could go wrong and what precautions will be implemented to minimise the risks identified? The specification of requirement may have highlighted some of the risks and may be seeking the views of the proposer on an appropriate strategy for dealing with them. However, the researcher will still need to consider any other risks not least because they may well have significant implications for the method, timetable and cost of the project. Both the stakeholder analysis and the risk assessment might lead the researcher to make initial enquiries or contacts to smooth the passage of the research. Stakeholder and risk analysis were the subject of Chapter 2.

Ethical issues resolved

It is a requirement when applying to ESRC and most other funders and commissioners of research for applicants to have considered the ethical issues surrounding their project. ESRC funding guidance states:

> Where ethical considerations arise in the design or conduct of the proposed research, applicants are asked to address these explicitly in their proposal.

And later:

> Applicants should demonstrate that full consideration has been given to
> the ethical implications of their research, and justify their means of
> resolving the ethical issues arising. If applicants are proposing to refer to a
> professional code of ethics governing research in their area, this should be
> specified and the appropriate part of the code appended to their application.

Ethical issues arising in social research are dealt with in greater depth in
Chapter 11.

Research design/methodology

Obviously all proposals need to state clearly how the research will be carried
out but more importantly why the chosen design is the appropriate approach
(and superior to others) in achieving the aims and objectives of the project.
In so doing it may be necessary to discuss alternative methodologies and
any experience you may have had of them. Primarily, the methodology needs
to be justified on scientific grounds but also on grounds of practicality and
cost-effectiveness.

Spell out also how the data (whether qualitative or quantitative) will be
analysed both in terms of the over-riding strategy and approach to be taken
and the specific data analysis techniques to be employed. It is also important
to relay how the analysis will provide answers to the research questions thus
linking analysis of the data to the aims and objectives of the project.

A specification of requirement may suggest a methodology for the project.
However, most funders would be receptive to alternative research designs if
convinced that it would lead to a better outcome from the research (that is, a
more scientifically robust result) or if the same output could be achieved at
less cost, in a shorter timescale or in a way that was less onerous to research
participants/data providers. Before proposing an alternative, the researcher
would be well advised to speak to the commissioner as there may be particular
reasons why a specific approach had been indicated.

Project plan and timetable

The proposal will need to include a sufficiently detailed plan to show how
the work will be undertaken, how the stages knit together and how this
fits into an overall and realistic timetable. The plan needs to highlight the
critical activities and the steps that will be taken to monitor progress and to
keep the project on track. The plan should also indicate 'who does what when',
linking the individual activities to the staff and other resources of the project
and stating how much time each person is to devote to each activity. This
will be especially important in a collaborative project where individuals or
organisations propose to work together on the project. Project planning is the
subject of Chapter 6.

Management structure

Who will lead the project, take overall responsibility and be ultimately accountable for the work? Make sure that person has allocated sufficient time to perform the task properly. The evidence suggests that Principal Investigators underestimate how much time is required in leading a project and feel they can combine this role with too many other duties. Routine management tasks, negotiations and quality-assuring the work take time, and there is always the unexpected to deal with.

Other management structures such as team meetings, internal reporting and procedures for ensuring quality need to be thought through. It is also important to include structures for liaising and engaging stakeholders, especially the commissioning or funding body.

Quality assurance

Funders are increasingly wanting to see procedures in place to ensure the quality of the work undertaken in the project. Points raised above about project management and minimising risk will be part of any quality plan. The quality plan will also depend on the nature of the project. Quality assurance is discussed in more detail in Chapter 8. Indicate who will write the report(s) and how that process is to be managed and quality assured – see Chapter 9 on dissemination.

Skills of team

It goes without saying that the team need to have the skills and experience to undertake the project to a high standard. However, simply appending CVs to the application is very rarely sufficient as they invariably take the form of one-line entries of posts held, previous research projects or grants held and publications. It is often difficult for those making funding decisions to appreciate the suitability of the researchers from such cryptic descriptions. A statement should be included which makes clear what knowledge, skills and previous experience the team has which is relevant to the project being proposed. Have the team (or members of it) worked with these stakeholders before? If so, describe the nature of that experience. Does the team have experience of the methodology and is it familiar with the data being collected? Has the team written reports for the commissioner before and is it possible to indicate from previous work their ability to write a satisfactory report this time?

Value for money/costings

Costs of the project will need to be estimated and presented. Funders issue instructions on what they are prepared to pay for and how they want the costs disaggregated by item of expenditure or type of activity. Financial aspects are discussed in the next section, however, it is important to emphasise here that adequate provision should be made for price changes that might occur through-out the project brought about by inflation or salary increases. Researchers often underestimate the costs involved in managing and quality-assuring a project and in liaising with funders by attending steering group or advisory group meetings. In a competitive market a balance has to be struck between obtaining generous resources to accommodate the unexpected while not being significantly undercut by the opposition. Nevertheless, if a fixed price contract is agreed the work will have to be completed for that price. One way of overcoming this problem is to present alternative costed options within a proposal; this may be appropriate when bidding for contracts, such as government contracts where no information is provided on the budget allocated for the project.

In the final reckoning the proposal will be judged on value for money not simply cost. So stand back, put yourself in the funder's position and ask yourself whether the work involved and the outputs from the project represent good value for the total cost of the project.

Additional comments on writing proposals

It is important to allow sufficient time for writing a proposal. Time will be required to consult with collaborators, assess options and to obtain stake-holders' support. And time will be needed to obtain all the necessary approval and signatures of the Head of the Department, Head of Finance or any other appropriate person within the organisation/institution. It is also important to quality-assure the proposal itself. In many circumstances time is of the essence as the commissioner may only have allowed three weeks for the preparation of a proposal.

Take steps to ensure that the proposal is well written and presented. It is not uncommon to hear funders say 'if the proposal itself is not well written it does not give us confidence that the final report will be well written'. Chapter 9 on dissemination discusses report writing and many of the points made there are also relevant to writing proposals.

Give thought to layout and presentation. In many cases the funder's application form will determine the information to be presented, the ordering of the information and so on. Nevertheless, bear in mind that any proposal may be photocopied (or printed if submitted on disk or electronically), faxed and widely circulated. Allow sufficient margins at the top, bottom and at each side, and think about numbering sections as well as pages. It is not unknown to receive a proposal where vital information has been lost through photocopying, most commonly the page numbers, which can lead to the proposal being reassembled in the wrong order.

Also be aware that many assessors of a proposal will not be experts in the field or will not have time to read the proposal in detail. Write in plain English and make sure that technical terms, if needed, are explained. Include clear summaries of the proposal, in prominent positions and clearly signposted.

Ask a colleague or friend to read the proposal to quality-assure it. Someone not involved in its production can read the proposal afresh and in a way the originator cannot. However, make sure that whoever performs this role is capable of doing it, and that does not just mean a person with the relevant knowledge and experience but someone whose relationship to you will not prevent them from being objective and appropriately critical.

Costing a project

When estimating the costs of a research project an applicant will need to ensure that the funds requested satisfy the following conditions:

- they are adequate to complete the work to the required standard
- they represent value for money
- they are competitive
- they fall within the funder's eligibility criteria
- they are disaggregaged and set out in a way that the funder requires.

Two points immediately stem from this list of conditions.

First, it is important to read the funding body's guidance on what items of expenditure they will meet and how they want the costs expressed in the application. Some funders place a ceiling on the amount they will grant for any one project.

Second, several of the conditions potentially conflict with each other. For example, a funder's eligibility criteria may preclude meeting certain costs and hence the full cost of the project. Making allowances for contingencies may increase costs to a level that makes the bid uncompetitive. A risk analysis is important here in order to gauge the financial implications of alternative scenarios. Furthermore, if the research sites have not been identified in advance, it may be difficult to estimate travel and subsistence expenses.

Eligibility

Research councils/ESRC

The ESRC will meet the full direct costs of the project apart from those associated with the permanent academic staff and premises. Thus it will meet the full staffing costs (salary, superannuation and national insurance) of those working on the project, including research assistants hired specifically for the project, and administrative, technical and secretarial support staff. The support staff may already be employed by the institution, but a proportion of their time will, in future, be devoted to the project. The ESRC will also meet the costs for replacement teaching in order to 'buy out' a permanent member of staff to work on the project if the work cannot be accommodated within existing commitments.

All travel and subsistence, which is incurred as a direct result of the project can be claimed as well as the cost of 'consumables' (equipment, stationery and photocopying, postage and phone calls, any specialist literature and software that needs to be acquired and attendance at specialist meetings or conferences to gain knowledge or gather vital information).

In addition, the ESRC will meet the costs of implementing the proposed dissemination strategy including arranging presentations to users and attendance at academic conferences to present findings. As a rule, the total costs for dissemination cannot exceed 5 per cent of the total cost of the project.

Although the ESRC will not meet indirect costs of the project, that is, the cost of the premises in which the researchers are located and all the infrastructure that is associated with it (library, central computer systems, finance and human resource support departments, etc.) the ESRC makes a contribution in the form of a standard rate, currently 46 per cent of the total direct staff costs (often referred to as 'institutional overheads'). However, the ESRC, along with all other research councils are changing to funding research on a 'Full Economic Cost' basis from late 2005. Applicants should check the ESRC website for details.

Charities

Broadly, charities will meet the direct costs of a project. They will *not* meet the costs of the time of the principal investigator if already in a salaried post and they will *not* pay institutional overheads. However, in meeting the direct costs of the project, they will pay for elements that would fall within institutional overheads under ESRC rules (such as rent, etc.) if they can be shown to have arisen solely, and as a direct result of the project. Charities will also contribute to the cost of publishing the report.

Government departments

Government departments are more flexible; their primary aim is to get the work done to the required standard at a price that represents good value for money. Because their research is competitively tendered and they (unlike the ESRC) can contract commercial research suppliers, they can accept costings set out in different ways. So, for example, a HE institution may bid setting out its costs in way similar to the ESRC (with staffing costs and institutional overheads) or a commercial company may list the staff to be engaged, the days each will work and the daily rate (which would include an element for institutional overheads).

Although government departments are more flexible they do need to judge different proposals on a comparative basis, so instructions in the specification of requirement may state how the costs are to be broken down, how unit costs are to be estimated and presented or a description of how the total cost has been arrived at. Government researchers are also fully aware of how other funders operate and what they accept and pay, so, for example, they will know the ESRC set institutional overheads at 46 per cent and are likely to query a proposal to them that included a significantly higher rate. Government departments can (and commonly do) negotiate over costs with a preferred supplier before signing a contract (see Chapter 5).

Points to consider

Think carefully about all costs that may arise and how they might vary over the course of the project. In a project spanning more than one year pay rises occur and staff will move up a position on a pay scale. Inflation can be expected to increase other costs over time, such as travel and subsistence. On the topic of travel and subsistence, be aware that they are not just incurred in fieldwork but also in attending start-up meetings, steering and advisory group meetings and when giving presentations.

When costing a proposal seek advice from experts within the organisation who have more extensive experience in these matters or who have responsibility for setting costs. They will know the institution's standard rates for travel and subsistence, pay, etc. and they will know what rates funders will pay. The ESRC will normally expect to pay salaries at points on established scales (either RA 1A or RA 1B) and these scales will be available from the HE finance or contracts department.

When bidding in response to an invitation, it is not always entirely clear from the specification of requirement the scope or nature of the project. In such circumstances it is advisable to present alternative costed proposals. The alternatives might be based on different methodological approaches or on different sample sizes or a different number of case studies. You may wish to propose additional, optional, components, which you feel are important and worthwhile and would considerably enhance the project. These should be costed separately. By costing individual components and alternative options, those judging the proposal are in a position to better assess the unit costs of the proposal and gauge its value for money.

It is also my experience that a specification of requirement most often does not list the research sites but rather states more generally that 'a range of prisons, schools (or whatever) will be selected at the start of the project' – according to some criteria – making it difficult to estimate travel and subsistence costs. In response to invitations from government departments I do not estimate a fixed cost in advance but state in my proposal that travel and subsistence will be incurred at the government department's standard rate and invoiced separately. I limit the amount to be claimed during the course of the project by stating that the total travel and subsistence will be no more than 10 per cent of the project cost – and any additional amount would fall to me to meet. Most government departments seem content with this arrangement and I have never known a project where 10 per cent was not sufficient (but I am thinking only of internal UK projects, not international comparative studies involving overseas travel).

VAT should not affect a competition as most funders accept that proposals should be compared exclusive of VAT (which they can, in any case, reclaim). Costs should therefore be submitted with VAT identified separately.

Ensuring safety of researchers working on the project may incur additional costs. If so, these need to be included. Budgeting for safety is discussed in Chapter 7.

Finally, the European Union reimburses costs in euros, so for researchers based outside the Euro zone, consideration needs to be given to exchange rates and likely changes in exchange rates.

Further guidance

Further advice and guidance on what to consider when preparing an application has been made available by funders. An example from each of the main sectors, research councils, charities and government departments can be found at:

www.esrc.ac.uk (enter *how to write a good application* in the search box)
www.jrf.org.uk/funding/research/applyforfunding/good.asp
www.dwp.gov.uk/asd/asad5/tendguide.pdf

Success rates

However good an application, success is not guaranteed. Quite the reverse, failure is a more likely outcome than success in applying for funding. Success rates for major funders are:

*   one in four applications to ESRC
*   one in five to government departments (because they usually invite five to bid)
*   one in twelve to European Union.

The vast majority of social researchers (probably all but I cannot prove that) have experienced failure, and probably a good deal of failure. So do not get into this game unless you are prepared for a constant level of rejection. And, believe me, the hurt from receiving news that a proposal one was passionate about, or had spent a considerable amount of time and effort preparing, has been rejected does not get any easier.

Get feedback but do not take it personally – learn the lessons (and sometimes there will not be any) and move on: seek alternative funding or abandon that one and get on to preparing the next proposal.

5 Negotiation to contract

Chapter 3 described the process of commissioning research and reached the point where the funder or customer for the research had identified a preferred supplier to undertake the research (subject to the successful resolution of any outstanding issues). From this point there follows a period of negotiation, which ultimately concludes with the signing of a contract. This period is sometimes referred to as *post-tender negotiations*.

Researchers more accustomed to applying for grants (where, it will be remembered a proposal is simply accepted or rejected) can find the negotiation stage a little daunting and confusing when working prescriptively to a customer's agenda. Dark suspicions arise that the commissioner wants to move the goalposts or reduce the cost. However, this is not normally the case. From the commissioner's point of view, he or she will have had a clear idea of what questions needed to be addressed when formulating the specification of requirement, and also some idea of the approach that might be taken. However, at the stage at which negotiations begin the commissioner will have read several proposals each suggesting slightly different ways to proceed. In addition, it will be the first time that the commissioner has really engaged with the details of how the work might be done. Furthermore, the research supplier may have offered alternative costed options and identified risks not previously acknowledged by the commissioner. In short there will always be issues to fine tune and clarify if not change.

Negotiation may be simply defined as a process through which parties move from their initially divergent positions to a point where agreement may be reached. Negotiation should be thought of as a potentially beneficial activity for both parties. Aim for 'win–win' where both sides feel that they have achieved some of what they wanted, otherwise one side is left feeling aggrieved and this may sour subsequent working relations. (And if one side is left wounded or betrayed they may seek to redress the balance at a later date.)

Even if there are not many thorny issues to discuss or resolve, negotiation can be valuable in that it is an opportunity for both sides to be assured of what is to be done and how it will be done. In this way the negotiation can be seen as a validation process where everyone can be made clear of his or her responsibilities from the outset. Furthermore, the initial negotiation might be the first meeting between the two sides and will begin to establish the nature of the ongoing working relationship. It is important, therefore, to approach the ensuing negotiation positively, constructively and openly.

How to negotiate

Most texts talk of the four-phased approach to negotiation: (1) preparation, (2) debate, (3) propose, and (4) bargain. However, it is seems more straightforward to collapse these into two:

- preparation – what you do before you meet the other side
- bargaining – what you do when you meet the other side.

Whichever schema is adopted it should be emphasised that negotiation is an iterative process. It is not common for every issue to be settled or agreed at the first meeting, invariably it requires several encounters with correspondence in-between. In a negotiation it is always possible to withdraw to reconsider the position, make preparations and return to continue the negotiation at a subsequent date.

Preparation

Thorough preparation prior to a meeting (or any other form of contact) is vital but it is all too often neglected or at least not undertaken to the extent that it should be. 'A negotiator who arrives poorly prepared is really only in a position to react to events, rather than lead them' (Kennedy, 1992).

At the preparation stage one needs to set *objectives* and to be absolutely clear what it is that one wants to achieve.

Also consider the *bottom line* or the walk-away point – the point below or at which the project becomes untenable either because it cannot be achieved in the timescale set or with resources available or because it would lack scientific credibility or validity.

Other issues can be see as *tradeables* that could be amended, compromised or exchanged without irreparably damaging the foundation or feasibility of the project. For example it may be possible to substitute case study B for the originally proposed case study of A, or both can be undertaken if additional resources are available. Further analysis could be undertaken if other data were made available and so on.

Identify the *fixed parameters* and *prioritise the tradeables*, that is, be clear of the fixed boundaries to the project but also what is not essential and can be offered.

Another useful exercise at this stage is to brainstorm what you think might be the *other side's position*. What do you think they want and how much do you think they value it, what is a priority for them and what might they be prepared to trade? How do their interests compare with yours?

In essence make sure you have done your homework before you begin to bargain.

Bargaining

Early in the meeting it is important to *formulate an agenda* and identify the issues that both sides wish to discuss. Often this can be done in advance by sending an email itemising the issues that you wish to discuss. The other party may respond by replying in advance of their concerns – they may have intimated this in their initial request for the meeting.

Always be prepared to *ask questions to clarify* the position and at regular intervals *summarise* where you think the discussions have reached. Before you make a response it is a good idea to summarise what they have proposed.

Always *trade concessions* in the form 'if . . . then', that is all offers are couched in conditional terms: if you will do x then we will do y.

When agreement has been reached take the earliest opportunity to prepare a *written record*. It might be possible to do this at the meeting, but, if not, as soon as you return to your office send an email saying, 'Thank you for the helpful meeting . . . My understanding is that we agreed a, b and c'. I do that even if the other side has agreed to prepare a note of the meeting. Leave nothing to chance as it is often the case that the other party moves on to another matter and any delay can lead memories to fade and ambiguity to enter. It does not matter if they prepare a note as well and the emails cross in cyberspace, the two will either confirm that both sides agreed on the decisions reached at the meeting or, if not, they will provide an early indication of what issues are still unresolved and need further deliberation.

It is important to *establish rapport* and empathy early on in the bargaining phase. Trust is an important requirement for a successful negotiation, not trickery. *Listen* to pick up the signals and cues. Be professional at all times and *avoid destructive debate*, attacking, blaming, point scoring, sarcasm and loss of temper. (I was once given the advice 'only lose your temper if you plan to do so'.) Always try to *make constructive suggestions*, do not simply complain. Remember, this is the start of a working relationship and getting off to a bad start will lessen the chances of a productive relationship later.

Textbooks discuss ploys that you or the other party might use to wrong foot one another or to gain an advantage. I will probably be considered naive or a 'soft touch' by seasoned negotiators, but it has been my experience that when discussing social research contracts, at least at the beginning of the project, neither side is seeking to pull a 'fast one' or to take an unfair advantage. The concern has only been to resolve any outstanding issues and to firm up the fine details. In view of this it is best to approach the negotiation positively and constructively rather than defensively or suspiciously. Negotiation textbooks also discuss different styles that one might adopt in conducting a negotiation and if the reader is likely to be involved in many negotiations or wishes to develop a style suitable for them, texts can readily be found on the management shelves of the university or local library.

If negotiations do not go well it is often because there is a lack of focus, usually because of inadequate preparation on the part of one side or the other or because of an absence of a clear agenda. Either way, confusion and ambiguity sets in resulting in antagonism as one side feels 'bounced'. The negotiation becomes more confrontational and acrimonious descending into the kind of destructive debate that one wishes to avoid. If such a situation is emerging withdraw on some pretext, and agree to reconvene if only in a few minutes' time. (Part of the preparation might be to think through how to withdraw in such circumstances, especially if you are negotiating as part of a team of colleagues. All will need to recognise the signals and respond collectively.)

Issues that often need to be negotiated and clarified

Leaving aside the issues that the commissioner may bring to the table (such as cost), the researcher should seek to clarify and agree the following matters before entering into a contract.

1   *Methodology*   Are both sides clear on the detailed methodology to be adopted? (A frequent contention is sample size, in particular whether it constitutes the number of subjects contacted or the number of achieved interviews.)
2   *Access*   Is it clear how access is to be obtained to the subjects of the research, data etc.?
3   *Timetables*   Has the project plan and the timing of the individual stages of the project been approved?
4   *Deliverables*   What is the researcher expected to deliver by way of data files, reports, presentations at meetings and so on? And how many and in what form?
5   *Acceptance criteria*   What criteria determine when the project has been satisfactorily completed? Most disputes are about whether or not the contractor has done the work to the standard agreed.
6   *Ownership*   Who owns the research instruments, the data and copyright of the reports? What constraints are there on publication, citation and dissemination?
7   *Procedures for resolving issues*   When the unexpected occurs what procedures need to be followed and what authority is required to make modifications to the plan?
8   *Responsibilities*   Who will make the initial contact with the subjects of the research (schools, NHS Trusts, prisons, or other stakeholders, data suppliers etc.) and who will be assigned as responsible for managing the contract on behalf of the commissioning body?
9   *Budget*   Has the budget been finalised and what is included and what is not included in the budget? What are the procedures for resolving concerns over budgeting?

The checklist of nine issues seems fairly obvious, but it is surprising just how often delays to a project, or at worst conflicts, arise over these very fundamental points. Given the multitude of reasons as to why events can go wrong with projects (discussed in Chapter 2) any steps that can be taken to prevent problems from arising should be taken. Resolving all these issues at the outset will pay handsome dividends later. As with any negotiation, once concluded it is important to get all decisions formalised in writing. Being the researcher in this situation it is certainly in my interest to reach agreement on such matters so I will initiate discussions and take a lead in producing a written record. (Although given the importance of having a clear written record of every offer made and decision taken, many government departments prefer, or even insist, that all post-tender negotiations are conducted in writing.) The record can be incorporated into any contract.

The contract

Once all issues have been resolved a contract can be drawn up. A contract is simply a legally binding agreement between two or more parties. Although contracts can be made orally or by the actions and conduct of the parties, in most cases they take the form of written documents. Written agreements have the obvious advantage of being less ambiguous and hence less prone to subsequent dispute. For a contract to be legally binding there must be an 'offer', which is a definite promise to be bound on certain terms and an 'unconditional acceptance'. If not all the terms of the offer are accepted then agreement has not been reached and the conditional acceptance is regarded as a 'counter offer'. Furthermore, to be a legal contract all parties must intend the agreement to be a legal one. (Intent differentiates legal contracts from other broad social arrangements.)

Note, an invitation to tender is not an offer but an invitation to the research supplier to make an offer. Also be wary of 'letters of intent' where the commissioner communicates that they wish you to do the work and will be offering you a contract. Letters of intent have been interpreted differently by the courts depending on the prevailing circumstances. Often they have been interpreted as having no legal meaning and as not a binding contract. For this reason they are not favoured by procurement specialists.

In English law the phrase 'time is of the essence' is of particular significance and if incorporated in a contract gives the customer the right to redress if the delivery date is not met. It is unusual to see such a clause in a social research contract as it is not always clear how the delay arose or whose fault it was. (It may be due to difficulties in gaining access, which is outside the control of both the commissioning body and the researcher.) However, some research councils (although not the ESRC) have begun to impose penalty clauses in their contracts, which lead to a loss of a certain percentage of the grant if the researcher is overdue in submitting a report.

Most government departments in particular, but also other large commissioners of research, will issue lengthy documents setting out the conditions of their contracts. Before signing make sure you fully understand what you are being committed to and that it unambiguously covers the checklist of points above. However, a contract need not be so wordy or detailed. I have conducted research for small organisations where we have exchanged letters, their letter saying what they want done and (after a negotiation) my letter in reply stating what I would do, how I would do it, by when and at what price. They have written back accepting my offer (which may have been modified in the light of a previous response). The essential elements are to commit to paper and ensure the paperwork covers all the issues that need to be agreed, including the liaison arrangements and the mechanism by which changes to the work can be raised and resolved during the life of the project.

Where research is being undertaken by a group of research organisations acting as a consortium – an increasingly common feature of current research (especially those involving large-scale evaluations of major government initiatives) – detailed attention should be given to the contractual arrangements. Consortia do not require different principles to be applied but they do make the contractual arrangements appreciably more complex. Before entering into such a contract be sure which organisations are responsible for what aspect of the work, to whom they are accountable and to whom they deliver what and when. Who is in the lead and who are the subcontractors? I have seen situations where the arrangements were not crystal clear enabling parties to renegotiate their responsibilities continuously throughout the duration of the project (and usually with a view to decreasing their input). The practice of most government departments is to only place one contract with the lead member of the consortium. It is then the lead member's responsibility to subcontract other members of the consortium.

Official Secrets Act 1989

Under the Official Secrets Act it is an offence to disclose certain official information if the disclosure is damaging to the national interest. The Act applies to Crown Servants, obviously, but less obviously to 'government contractors', including anyone who is not a Crown Servant but who provides or is employed in the provision of goods or services for the purpose of a Minister. Anyone working on a research contract with a government department is therefore affected by the Act and bound by its provisions. Official information is deemed to be any information, document or article which the person has in his or her possession by virtue of his or her position as a contractor. It is also an offence not to take reasonable care of the document to prevent the unauthorised disclosure, to retain it contrary to official duty or for the contractor to fail to comply with an official direction for the return or disposal of the information.

In undertaking research for government the contractor may be given confidential information but it is unlikely that unauthorised disclosure would be interpreted by the courts as 'damaging to the national interest', although disclosure might well be damaging to an individual or an organisation.

Nevertheless, the Act does alert researchers to the need to handle information appropriately. At the start of a project government departments do provide researchers working on their contracts with a basic guide to the Act and request them to sign a form saying that they have received the guide and understand that they are bound by the Act.

Further negotiations

In this chapter negotiation has been discussed in the context of determining the scope of the work and drawing up a contract. But negotiations will take place throughout the life of the project with various stakeholders, to gain access to data and so on. The general comments made above on how to negotiate (how to prepare and how to bargain) apply equally to all other situations. Understanding the negotiation process and having skills at negotiation are therefore extremely important for a project manager.

Of course negotiation is not the only means of arriving at a decision and negotiation may well be an inappropriate procedure on occasions. Among the functions that a research manager has to perform are directing and controlling the project and often decisions do not need to be negotiated, but clear and unambiguous instructions need to be issued.

6 Project planning

Plans will be needed to estimate the time and resources required to complete the proposed project to the required quality. Plans also determine how the project will proceed – 'who does what when'. In more detail, devising and agreeing a plan involves a variety of actions, including:

- agreeing objectives and quality standards
- listing activities
- estimating start times and durations for each activity
- identifying dependencies between activities
- constructing a schedule
- identifying the critical path(s)
- nominating milestones
- itemising resources
- formulating responsibilities.

Note that an initial plan may need several revisions before a final plan emerges, this is because various options or constraints will present themselves and choices or compromises will be needed.

The steps to be taken and the tools that can be used to plan a project are best explained by way of an example. The example chosen here is a study of drug treatment programmes for offenders serving prison sentences who experience drug problems. The study was reported in Burrows *et al.* (2001) and is described briefly below.

Example: Drug treatment programmes for offenders

The joint aims of the study were to describe the nature of drug treatment programmes for prisoners with drug misuse problems and gauge the impact of interventions on offenders' behaviour following release. To meet this remit, the study was conceived in terms of two broadly distinct strands: one descriptive and the other evaluative. From a descriptive perspective the objective was to identify how drugs-related treatment programmes prepare prisoners for release and what kind of help they receive on their return to the community. The purpose behind the evaluative focus was to gain an insight into the short-term impact of treatments and procedures on ex-prisoners' drug-taking behaviour and criminal activity. A key feature of the overall research design was to 'track' a cohort of released prisoners for up to four months after their release.

The project was to start in January of Year 1, run for eighteen months and finish at the end of June in Year 2. In actual fact, as is often the case, the start was delayed by one month until February but the completion date was not put back correspondingly. It thus became a seventeen-month project.

A broad quality standard was associated with each aim. First, the research was to obtain a comprehensive picture of the range of programmes in existence throughout the country addressing the drug misuse problems of prisoners. Second, as large as possible a number of prisoners were to be included in the tracking exercise (there was no sampling frame to draw on) and sample attrition between completing the first and second questionnaire was to be minimised.

The descriptive strand

As part of the preliminary fieldwork the research team carried out interviews with the 'principal authorities' in the field of treatment for offenders with drugs problems. A number of individuals and organisations were approached. These included those prisons and probation services, identified by members of the project Steering Group and others, as being 'advanced' in their treatment procedures; drug services involved in delivering treatment; and research organisations who had carried out tracking studies or similar work. Those consulted were also stakeholders in the project and the exercise provided an opportunity to conduct a detailed stakeholder analysis.

In consultation with the Steering Group, the research team identified seventeen institutions for in-depth study and for the implementation of the tracking exercise. The seventeen were selected from the sixty-three establishments running drug treatment pilot schemes and were chosen to reflect a variety of treatment programmes (for example, detoxification, counselling, education) run by different service providers and to a range of different prisoners (young, old, male, female, short-term and long-term prisoners).

As well as visiting these institutions to set up the tracking mechanisms, members of the research team also observed the drug treatment programme and interviewed members of staff involved in the delivery of the programmes. The visits gathered information on the range of services provided in terms of their scope, size, management and how prisoners' needs were identified and the procedures by which prisoners were referred to the scheme or selected for it. Professionals were also invited to identify what they considered to be good practice in treating offenders' drugs problems.

In order to complement the institutional perspective, focus groups and interviews were held with inmates who had experience of drugs-related treatment from a previous custodial sentence. Focus groups of between six and ten inmates and individual interviews were held in eight of the seventeen institutions participating in the study. The purpose of the exercise was to explore inmates' views about access to drug services within the prisons where they had been incarcerated, identify what preparations had been made for their release and discover if their return to prison was in any way connected with their continued misuse of drugs. The focus groups and interviews also provided an opportunity to discuss the problems faced by prisoners with a history of drug misuse when they are released into the community.

The evaluative strand

The tracking of a cohort of prisoners following their release from prison formed a major component of the study. In order to inform the shape and content of the tracking exercise a review of research studies that had attempted tracking drug users in the community was undertaken. Respondents in this study were required to complete one questionnaire shortly before their release from prison and a second questionnaire three to four months later following their release into the community. Clearly, tracking individuals who have had any contact with the criminal justice system represents a major challenge especially if they had chaotic lifestyles as a result of drug dependency.

A number of steps were taken in response to the predicted high sample attrition rate. To encourage continued participation following release from prison, on completion of the second questionnaire offenders received a fee of £20. In addition, prisoners were asked to complete a written consent form as part of the first questionnaire, so as to overcome any problems concerning confidentiality that might arise when members of the research team contacted field probation officers and drug agency staff as part of the follow-up exercise. At the time of completing the first questionnaire, inmates were also asked to provide up to four addresses where they could be contacted following their release from prison. Finally, for those respondents who were to be supervised by the Probation Service following release, a copy of the follow-up questionnaire was also sent to the supervising probation officer with a request that it be handed on to the client.

The first questionnaire was designed to cover a number of issues including self-reported drug use prior to imprisonment, the type of drug treatment received while in prison and the help given within prison with regard to obtaining treatment or support in the community. Respondents were asked to give details of their drug use in the thirty days prior to imprisonment. This required them to name the drug(s) taken during this period, provide an estimate of how much money they spent on drugs in a typical week and state how they raised the money to pay for the drugs.

The second questionnaire, which was sent out approximately four months after the prisoner's discharge date, was designed to elicit information about drug use both before and after release from prison. There were also questions dealing with employment status, living arrangements, the type of community drug services used since leaving prison and involvement in criminal activity.

Activities

Having described the design of the study it is possible to break the work down into a set of discrete tasks or activities and to estimate the time each activity is expected to take. The information is presented in Table 6.1.

In estimating the time each activity is expected to take, it is recommended to use units of time that seem most appropriate. In some instances it might be suitable to express time in days, in others, weeks. Here, taking months as the unit seems adequate even through some of the activities were estimated in smaller units and aggregated. For example, it was estimated that an average of five working days would be needed for each site visit and as prisons could be visited in any order that seventeen weeks rounded up to five months (to allow for some contingencies) seemed sufficient time to complete this activity. Note, duration is the time between starting the activity and finishing it, regardless of whether one is working on it full-time, part-time or hardly at all. Consider for example the second activity listed in Table 6.1, 'selection of a subset of prisons'. It did not take two months to identify the prisons we wished to include in the study, far from it. But we did need to allow two months to write to governors of the prisons notifying them of our intentions, explain the project and answer their (or more usually their staffs') queries, establish contact with the relevant staff, reach agreement and negotiate access.

Table 6.1 Drug treatment programmes for offenders: project activities, durations and persons assigned to undertake them

Activity	Duration (months)	Persons assigned
Review data/key players	2.0	PI & SR
Selection of a subset of prisons	2.0	PI & SR
Develop research instruments for site visits	1.0	SR & RA1
Develop research instruments for tracking exercise	1.0	SR & RA1
Site visits to prisons	5.0	SR & RA1
Sample prisoners and issue first questionnaire	4.0	Prison staff
Issue second questionnaire	5.0	RA2
Analyse institutional responses from site visits	1.0	SR & RA1
Analyse data from focus groups/interviews with prisoners	1.0	SR & RA1
Analyse data from first questionnaire	1.0	SR & RA2
Analyse data from second questionnaire	1.0	SR & RA2
Write report(s)	3.0	PI & SR

Key: PI, Principal Investigator; SR, Senior Researcher; RA1, First Research Assistant; RA2, Second Research Assistant; Prison staff, anyone located at the prison who is involved in the drug treatment programme (e.g. Prison Officers, Agency staff running the programme)

Initially it is best to be conservative in the time allowed for an activity. Remember the maxim 'expect the unexpected'. Some project management texts suggest estimating a minimum and maximum time then using these to produce a best and worst case scenario. However, in social research the worst case might extend the project indefinitely, perhaps because the data is not available or access cannot be gained to research subjects. The risk analysis should have identified possible difficulties and delays and these can be used to produce a conservative (but not worst case) estimate.

Dependencies

Individual activities have been listed in Table 6.1. Because it is often most convenient when identifying activities to think of them as they will occur during the project life cycle they have been listed in Table 6.1 in an approximate sequence of occurrence. Of course, some activities can only begin when others have been completed; to take an obvious example, data cannot be analysed until it has been collected. The analysis stage is thus *dependent* on the data having been assembled. Other activities can be undertaken simultaneously, that is, in parallel with each other. In this example the information collected from the site visits can be analysed and written up at the same time that the tracking exercise is in the field.

Dependencies need to be identified so that the work can be scheduled. A well-established method of scheduling project activities is by constructing a Gantt chart.

Gantt chart

The Gantt chart is named after the Belgian industrialist, Henri Gantt, who devised the methodology around the time of the First World War. It is very simple in its conception, being a two-way table or matrix with activities occupying the rows along the vertical axis and time expressed along the horizontal axis. It may take several iterations to arrive at a final and workable schedule, especially when costs and resources are factored in. For example, if only one person works on the project and performs all the tasks, the length of the project will be the length of time it takes to undertake all activities (although there may be some savings if all the tasks do not require the person to be engaged full-time). In the example above the total sum of all activities is twenty-seven months, which is ten months longer than the time allowed for the project.

Two Gantt charts for the drug treatment project are shown in Figures 6.1 and 6.2. The first is the initial Gantt chart, the second is the final Gantt chart adopted for the project.

For each activity the earliest start date is indicated together with the duration. So, in Figure 6.1, activity 'review data/key players' can begin on Day 1 of the project (1 February), it is expected to take two months to complete and thus be finished by the end of March. The second activity, 'select subset of prisons', cannot begin until the first activity is completed (because the initial discussions inform the selection of prisons). The second activity can begin at the earliest on 1 April and end 31 May. The third and fourth activities are to develop research instruments needed for later stages of the project. However, they can be started, in theory (leaving aside resource constraints) on 1 April. (Not before as their development needs to be informed by the initial discussions.) 'Dev instruments for visits' can be started 1 April but need not be completed until 1 June when the visits take place, that is, two months later. As they only take one month to develop there is one additional (spare) month to complete the work. Likewise tracking instruments are not required until November so there are six spare months to complete their development. 'Site visits' (activity 5) however, cannot begin until the prisons have been selected (activity 2).

Additional or spare time to complete an activity is called *float* in the UK and *slack* in the USA.

The convention when drawing Gantt charts is to start at the earliest start time and draw a continuous line for the duration. Any float (or slack) is depicted by a dotted line. However, the technology available to Mr Gantt in the early part of the twentieth century has long since been superseded and better options are available, especially as different aspects of the chart can be presented in different colours, greatly adding to their clarity and impact. Here a Word table has been constructed, xxx used to represent duration and — to indicate float.

For every project there will be at least one (in some cases more than one) *critical path*. The critical path is the set of activities that must be undertaken in sequence and the sum of those activities is the minimum time in which the

Year 1 (columns calendar months) Year 2

Activity	F1	M1	A1	M1	J1	J1	A1	S1	O1	N1	D1	J2	F2	M2	A2	M2	J2	J2	A2	S2	O2
Review data/key players	xxx	xxx																			
Select subset of prisons			xxx	xxx																	
Dev instruments for visits			xxx	—	—	—	—	—													
Dev instruments for tracking			xxx	—	—	—	—	—	—												
Site visits to prisons					xxx	xxx	xxx	xxx	xxx												
Sample pris/issue 1st quest										xxx	xxx	xxx	xxx								
Issue 2nd quest											—	—	xxx	xxx	xxx	xxx	xxx	xxx			
Analyse data from site visits										xxx	—	—	—	—	—	—	—				
Analyse data from prisoners										xxx	—	—	—	—							
Analyse data from 1st quest														xxx	—						
Analyse data from 2nd quest																		xxx			
Write report																			xxx	xxx	xxx

Figure 6.1 Initial Gantt chart for the drug treatment programmes for offenders project

Year 1 (columns calendar months)   Year 2

Activity	F1	M1	A1	M1	J1	J1	A1	S1	O1	N1	D1	J2	F2	M2	A2	M2	J2
Review data/key players	XXX	XXX			ms1			ms2				ms3				ms4	
Select subset of prisons			XXX	—													
Dev instruments for visits			XXX	—	—												
Dev instruments for tracking			XXX	—	—												
Site visits to prisons					XXX	XXX	XXX										
Sample pris/issue 1st quest								XXX	XXX	XXX	XXX						
Issue 2nd quest											XXX	XXX	XXX	XXX	XXX		
Analyse data from site visits								XXX	—	—	—	—	—	—	—	—	
Analyse data from prisoners								XXX	—	—	—	—	—	—	—	—	
Analyse data from 1st quest												XXX	—	—	—	—	
Analyse data from 2nd quest																XXX	
Write report													XXX	—	—	—	XXX

Figure 6.2 Final Gantt chart for the drug treatment programmes for offenders project

project can be completed. The critical path has been tinted in Figures 6.1 and 6.2. Activities on the critical path are important because any delay in starting those activities or any overrun in completing them will add to the total project time. Note that is because activities on the critical path have no float, unlike all other activities which do, and hence there is some flexibility as to when they are undertaken. (An alternative definition of the critical path is those activities that do not have any float.)

It can be seen from the initial Gantt chart, Figure 6.1, that, as scheduled, the programme would not be completed until the end of October Year 2, some four months after the specified end date. In planning the project the question thus becomes how could four months be saved without compromising the quality of the project? Obviously savings in the overall time can only stem from savings in completing activities on the critical path.

Considering the activities on the critical path, it quickly became apparent that no savings could be made on the activities 'sample prisoners/issue 1st quest' because it had been estimated (as best it could) that to obtain a sufficiently large sample of prisoners passing through treatment programmes and being released from prison, all those meeting both criteria in the four-month period were needed. Similarly, the follow-up period 'issue 2nd quest' had to be five months because a minimum of three months had to elapse before the second questionnaire could be issued (and allowance had to be made for chasing up non-responders).

The estimated duration for 'review data/key players', 'select subset of prisons' and 'analyse data from 2nd quest' (other activities on the critical path) left little room for manoeuvre, which left only 'site visits to prisons' and 'write report' as potential candidates for time savings. Given each prison visit only required five working days (one week), savings could be made by assigning more than one person to this activity. It was thus decided to reduce the length of this activity from five to three months by assigning two people to visit prisons. Turning to the report, its preparation did not need to be left until the end of the project. Large sections of the report could be written much earlier in the project life cycle as certain aspects of the research were concluded. (Report writing is discussed further in Chapter 9 Dissemination where it will be strongly recommended that report writing is undertaken as early as possible and not left until the last minute. In fact, 'write report' was only left at the end of this project in Figure 6.1 to illustrate the way time might be saved on a project.)

Amendments to the two activities 'site visits to prisons' and 'write report' enabled the project to be brought within the seventeen-month timescale. The final schedule is depicted in Figure 6.2.

A criticism levelled at Gantt charts is that they do not represent the schedule clearly or unambiguously when there are many activities with a high degree of interdependency between them. In such situations PERT (programme evaluation and review technique) diagrams are considered to be a better method. However, for the most part, social research projects are not sufficiently complex in structure that the move to PERT methodology is necessary and so it is not described here. Readers wishing to be informed of PERT should consult any detailed project management text such as Field and Keller (1998).

Milestones

Milestones are key points or stages in the course of the project and they are marked by some tangible outcome or deliverable. They are interim goals that can be used to signify the progress of the project. In social research milestones might include *completed data collection*, or *written report* and so on. Milestones are considered to be more useful for monitoring the progress of a project, to see that the key stages have been reached on time. They are not considered so useful for planning or scheduling the detailed activities. For this reason it is advisable not to have either too few or too many milestones as either minimises their impact. Too few invariably places too much time between the major stages which can then be forgotten or lost while the work is progressing, if designating too many they become more akin to weekly reports of work done. The accepted wisdom is that there should be between five and fifteen milestones depending on the size of the project.

In the drugs treatment project, five milestones suggest themselves:

Milestone 1   End May/early June Year 1: complete initial set-up phase
At this point all the discussions to clarify the project, select and seek agreement of prisons should have been finalised. In addition, all research instruments should have been developed or at an advance stage of development. Data collection can begin.

Milestone 2   End September/early October Year 1: complete visits to prisons, initiate tracking
At this point all prisons should have been visited and information gathered about their treatment programmes. Furthermore, the sampling of prisoners and the issuing of questionnaires should have started at this point and confirmation can be sought that this component is proceeding satisfactorily.

Milestone 3   June Year 2: sampling of prisoners completed and follow-up questionnaires being issued
At this point the number of prisoners sampled will be known and their completed questionnaires can be coded. Any teething troubles in issuing the second questionnaires will have been resolved and the tracking exercise will be underway. Also at this stage, data from the earlier fieldwork should have been analysed and preparation of the report should be at an advanced stage.

Milestone 4 May Year 2: complete data collection
By this time all data should have been successfully collected. The end of the project should be in sight.

Milestone 5   End June Year 2: project completed

A good final report should have been written and submitted to the sponsor. (Strictly, as milestones mark the achievement of interim goals, purists would say that one should not be at the end of the project to mark the achievement of the final goal. However, while it may not be a milestone, more a winning post, I believe reaching the ultimate objective should be marked and celebrated in some way.)

Milestones can be indicated on the Gantt chart and (with the exception of milestone 5) they are shown on the final plan for the project at Figure 6.2.

Although the prime purpose of milestones is to mark the completion of the main phases of the project 'along the way', they are beginning to assume greater significance with funders who are increasingly tying interim payments to milestones by which a certain amount of funds will be paid when each milestone is reached. The milestones and the amount to be paid is invariably stated in the contract. This approach, it is felt, links payment more closely to results and outcomes during the project and is preferable to simply releasing funds after a certain period of time has elapsed regardless of what has been achieved during the time period.

Itemising resources and assigning responsibilities

Having considered activities, how they relate and need to be scheduled, the next stage is to consider who will undertake those activities and what other resources will be required. The greatest resource on a social research project is people, the researchers, so the major issue to resolve is 'who does what when'.

In most projects, the principal investigator and one other collaborator will be known at the outset as they are the ones initiating the project or wishing to respond to a specification of requirement. They will also have some indication of the time that they can devote to the project, given their other commitments. Academics undertake research alongside teaching and other administrative responsibilities and professional researchers are often juggling their time between more than one research project. The question then becomes what additional skills will be required to complement their own and what other assistance do they need to undertake the work that they will not have time to do? Others will thus need to be recruited to the project. Whether or not the individuals have been identified at the start, it is important to assign a person or persons to each activity.

Like scheduling, it may take several iterations to bring activities and responsibilities into line. People may only be able to commit to the project at certain times, there are only so many working hours in a day, people cannot be in two places at once and so on.

In the drugs treatment project the Principal Investigator (PI) and the Senior Researcher (SR) together initiated the project and intended to lead the project and contribute significant time to it. A further researcher (SR2) was available to work part-time on the project and took responsibility for liaising with prisons. SR2's other tasks were to encourage prisons to issue questionnaires to prisoners, code data from the first questionnaire and send out the second questionnaire at the appropriate time. In addition, SR2 logged second questionnaires, sent out reminders if they were not returned and coded data on receipt of a questionnaire. It quickly became apparent that further assistance would be needed to visit prisons, especially when the time allocated for this element had to be shortened in order to stay within the overall time limit placed on the project. Another researcher (SR1) was sought and engaged to help with the data collection from prisons and with the analysis of that data. The allocation of responsibilities to tasks is shown in the final column of Table 6.1.

Simply assigning activities to persons working on the project is not the end of the planning stage. The plan needs to be validated. It can be seen from the Gantt chart, Figure 6.2, that the SR is under pressure in April and September of Year 1 when he or she is scheduled to work on more than one activity. However, this should not prove a problem as all the activities that SR has to undertake have float, that is, there is some flexibility as to when they need to be done. The Gantt chart could be amended to bring resources, activities and time into harmony, but it was felt not to be necessary here, the pressure points were noted and itemised for project meetings.

A further complication may arise when those involved are working on other projects at the same time. In such situations it may be necessary to validate the project plan for one project against the plan for another. It is even possible (although not usually worth the effort) to have a master plan, which has as its activities individual projects.

Having concluded who does what when it is important to draw up a responsibility chart, a diary, calendar or what ever seems to fit the situation best which clearly indicates to each person on the project how much time they need to commit to the project, when they need to commit that time (that is, be on the project) and what specifically they will be doing when engaged on the project.

So far only human resources have been mentioned, but other resources will be needed, such as office premises and the resources attached to them (phones, computer hardware and software, paper and photocopiers, etc.). Such resources are invariably provided by the host institution, but some internal negotiation may be needed to ensure their availability at the appropriate time.

Before concluding project planning it is important to stand back from the plan and consider whether it looks appropriate and plausible. When developing plans a bottom-up approach is taken and that has been the approach taken so far. As a final validation of the plan consider it in its entirety, that is, top-down. Ask if it is really possible to complete that kind of project, with all that it entails within that timescale? It can be possible by piecing together individual activities to arrive at an overall plan that is not feasible. Conversely the bottom-up approach may fail to spot opportunities for economies and savings and lead to an unnecessarily long timescale.

Microsoft Project 2000

Software exists to aid the development of project plans. In the past software has been complex and not easy to use and expensive to buy, thus while in common usage in industry it has been beyond the reach of most social researchers who have got by with manual tools. That now has changed with the availability of Microsoft Project 2000, which is relatively cheap and easy to use. It may be a useful tool for those planning and managing many projects, which involve a variety of activities and engage several people. I would not recommend such software to plan a literature review to be undertaken by one person.

Like all packages, some time has to be invested in training and learning how to use it. Once one understands the principles, theory and terminology of project planning, Microsoft Project 2000 is easy to pick up. The manual is very clear and a trip to the local library will reveal a plethora of self instruction books. I found Murphy (2001) particularly helpful. It is not the intention here to describe Microsoft Project in detail or to provide instruction on how to use it, but simply to describe its basic features, which may help the reader decide whether investment in learning the package would be worthwhile.

Entering Microsoft Project brings up a screen inviting the user to input the different project activities and the estimated duration of the activity. The units of time can be hours, days, months or whatever the user thinks appropriate and it is possible to use the zoom facility to display charts and diagrams in greater or lesser time detail. Unless otherwise indicated, Microsoft Project assumes every activity will begin on day 1, which is taken to be tomorrow when one is inputting. In order to agree with the dates in the drug treatment example (Figure 6.2), a start date of February 2005 was used. Having entered the activities it is straightforward to establish dependencies by clicking on the two activities and then clicking on the symbol of a chain link on the tool bar.

Down the left hand side of the screen is the View Bar. Clicking on 'Gantt Chart' immediately displays the Gantt chart for the project. This option has been chosen and is displayed below in Figure 6.3. The default is to display activities on the critical path in one colour and activities not on the critical path in another. In order to be able to distinguish them in black and white, solid black has been chosen to represent the critical path and open boxes activities that are not critical.

Next to each activity can be entered the person who will undertake the activity (or details of any other resources that will be required) and the amount of time each person has available. This has not been shown on the example here but is a simple matter of scrolling to the left-hand part of the screen that lists activities to reveal further columns for data entry. Costs of resources can also be incorporated.

It can be seen from the screen that the View Bar contains other options for displaying the data. They are:

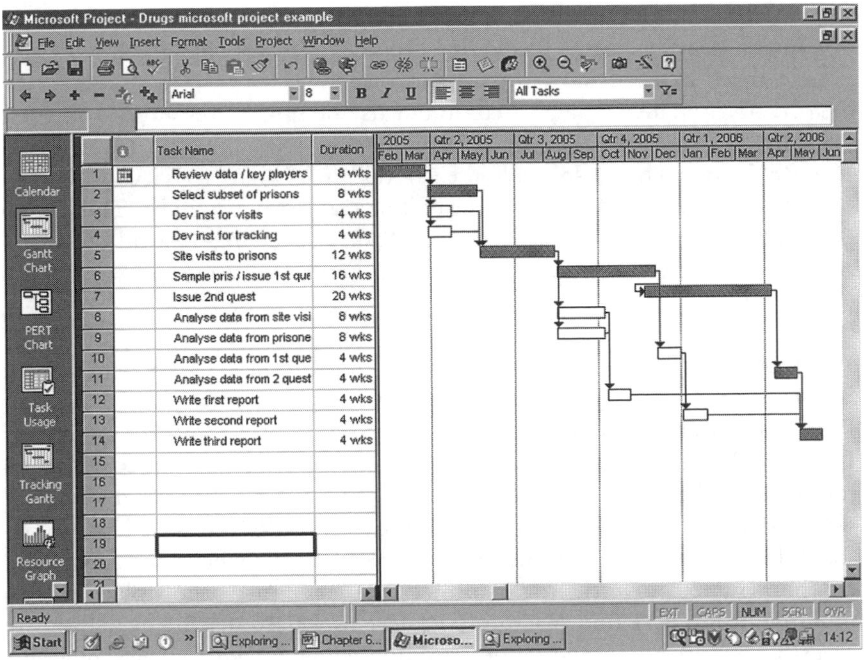

Figure 6.3 Screen from Microsoft Project 2000 showing Gantt chart for drug
treatment programmes for offenders research project

Calendar This simply produces a calendar showing each day what activity is
scheduled to be in progress.

Gantt Chart This displays the Gantt chart. The Gantt chart can display a lot
more information than shown in the example above. Milestones, float
(or slack) and the names of the person(s) undertaking the work or other
resources can be included. However, this can make the Gantt chart very
cluttered. I personally prefer to keep displays simple and clear. The other
information can be presented on other outputs.

PERT Chart This constructs a PERT network diagram. (PERT methodology,
it was mentioned earlier, is not discussed in this book.)

Task Usage This screen shows for each activity which resources will be
deployed on them, how much of each resource is required and when it will
be needed.

Tracking Gantt For any project plan, a Baseline Gantt can be saved, to show
how the project is intended to progress. Once underway the actual time
taken to complete an activity can be inserted and a revised Gantt chart
produced. Comparing the two reveals whether the project is ahead of
schedule, on target or slipping. Tracking Gantt displays the two Gantts
in different colours to highlight any deviations from the plan.

Resource Graph This graphically displays for each resource the percentage of
time it is committing each day. This option is useful for ascertaining

whether a resource is over-committed on any particular day (shown in red). In the drugs example, 'Resource Graph' indicates that the SR is over-stretched in April and September of Year 1.

Resource Sheet   This displays a complete list of project resources and their costs.

Resource Usage   This displays for each resource what activity it will be undertaking, when and what the cost of that resource will be. This option contains the same information as 'Task Usage' but instead of listing resources and cost within each activity it lists activity and cost within each resource.

Whether the investment in time and effort to learn the software is well spent is contested. I know of two organisations that have introduced Microsoft Project only to have discontinued its use some time later. However, from what I know of their experience, the package was introduced for all project planning regardless of the size and complexity of the project. Furthermore, the package was used almost as an administrative record of projects that were being sponsored. In my view, the software only becomes valuable when used and owned by the principal investigator or project manager to develop plans and to monitor progress. I find Microsoft Project especially useful in helping to identify pressure points and for determining who does what when. To be able to clearly indicate when people need to make themselves available to the project, what proportion of their time is required and what they are expected to do removes a good deal of uncertainty and avoids confusion later.

7 Research staff

Colleagues, collaborators, research and administrative staff are the main resources of any research enterprise. They bring inspiration, innovation and the technical and intellectual know-how. If the team gels, the experience of working on the project is pleasurable, enjoyable and intellectually stimulating. People also represent by far and away the largest cost of any project.

Team members may already be in post to undertake the research. They may have designed the study and been named in the proposal. On the other hand, it is often the case that new staff need to be recruited, either specifically for a project or more generally, to increase the staffing complement of the research organisation. For the benefit of researchers seeking employment opportunities, academic posts (teaching as well as research) are advertised at www.jobs.ac.uk. The Education supplement of the *Guardian*, which is published on Tuesdays, and the *Times Higher Educational Supplement* also contain an extensive coverage of research posts in academia. The Society supplement in Wednesday's *Guardian* is a good source for research jobs in central and local government, local authorities, charities and commercial social research/survey companies/ private research agencies. Many groups advertise vacancies at their own websites. For example, vacancies in Government Social Research can be found at www.gsr.gov.uk. Members of the Social Research Association (SRA) are notified electronically of posts coming to the SRA's attention.

Employment law

The purpose here is not to give a textbook account of employment law but to highlight the issues that need to be thought through and clarified in any research project. Should research managers require further details on how the law applies they can be found in many employment law texts (for example, Lockton, 2003).

The Employment Rights Act 1996 states that 'employee means an individual who has entered into or works under a contract of employment'. In the vast majority of cases it will be clear who is the employee and who is the employer. Researchers in higher education institutions, public bodies, market research companies and large research organisations will have been recruited through open competition and will have been offered a contract of employment which they have signed. The contract, which by law the employer must give to the employee within two months of the start of employment, will set out the terms and conditions and nature of the employment.

Note that two significant groups are not employees. First, the large number of research students located in academic institutions are not employees of that institution. (Some may well be employed by other organisations and are registered as part-time students of the university.) Research students have a grant to finance their studies, not a wage, and their work is supervised rather than line managed by their employer. (To this extent they have more autonomy and greater freedom of choice than employed contract researchers.) The second group is the growing number of self-employed social researchers.

Entering into a contract of employment places obligations on employers, in effect to comply with four implied terms. These are:

1   a duty to pay wages (and deduct tax and National Insurance)
2   a duty to provide grievance procedures
3   a duty of mutual trust and confidence
4   a duty to exercise reasonable care with regard to health and safety.

The first two are self-explanatory and are not discussed further here.

The duty of mutual trust and confidence has been defined by the court as an obligation that the employer should not 'without reasonable and proper cause, conduct [him/herself] in a manner calculated to or likely to destroy or seriously damage the relationship of confidence and trust between employer and employee'.

The standard of care expected of the employer has been defined by the court as 'the care which an ordinary prudent employer would take in all the circumstances'. Major employers will be well aware of their duties regarding health and safety as it relates to their own offices and premises. However, social research often entails the researcher being away from the office to conduct fieldwork, gather data and so on. The employer's obligation extends to all situations in which the employee may be placed as part of their employment (in this case research) duties. Regulations introduced in 1993 following an EC Directive (89/391) impose a duty on employers to conduct a risk assessment exercise to examine all risks that the employee faces and to put into practice appropriate preventative measures to eradicate or to minimise those risks. As the research manager or principal investigator would be expected to undertake this risk assessment on behalf of the employing organisation, as well as assuming a general ethical responsibility to ensure the safety of the research team, safety of research staff is considered in detail later in this chapter.

Employees have rights to redundancy payments, statutory notice periods, holidays and time off and not to be unfairly dismissed.

The obligations are not just one way, the employee has duties to the employer. One, of course, is to honour the expressed terms of the contract. Not to do so would constitute a breach of contract. However, there are other, implied terms such as obedience and adaptability under which an employee should obey all reasonable and lawful orders (but not those that would lead to an illegal act or which would place the employee in immediate danger). The employee should also adapt to new methods of working introduced by the employer (although there is an obligation on the employer to provide appropriate training). In addition, the employee has a duty to exercise reasonable care in carrying out his/her work and not to cause injury to a third party. Finally, the employee has a duty of fidelity or good faith towards the employer, that is, to cooperate and not to compete with the employer whilst in his or her employment.

Two other issues are resolved by the employer/employee relationship. First, vicarious liability rests with the employer such that an employer is responsible for the legal consequences of any actions on the part of the employee undertaken in the course of the work. Second, copyright of any work created by an employee in the course of his or her official duties at work is owned by the employer. (Copyright is discussed in more detail in Chapter 10.)

When an employment relationship exists, responsibilities on the part of the employer and employee are clear and covered by employment law developed through statute, common law and set out in the terms of the employment contract. However, social research often entails entering into different collaborative working relationships with other researchers, groups or organisations who come together to work jointly, in order to complement each other's skills or because they share a common research interest. One researcher or organisation may be in the lead, another engaged on a particular basis or for a specific assignment (for example, to extract data, conduct interviews, run focus groups, or provide specialist advice on complex statistical analysis). Under these arrangements matters become more complex, especially if one or more of the researchers are self-employed or are independent contractors who are not generally covered by the same employment laws.

Whereas employees are engaged under a contract of employment, in essence a *contract of service*, those who are self-employed and operate as an independent contractor are engaged under a *contract for services*. Not being employed, employment law does not apply to self-employed independent contractors. All that applies are the terms of the contract made for their services. Hence any contract should address those issues that would otherwise be covered by a contract of employment had there existed an employer–employee relationship.

Before highlighting the issues, a further word is needed on the distinction between an employee and a self-employed person. Whether a person is employed or self-employed is not simply a matter for the parties to agree. The courts can decide and have applied various tests to determine whether a person should be regarded as an employee, but a description of these tests is outside the scope of this book. The system of taxation is also different for employed and self-employed people leading the Inland Revenue to take a keen interest in these matters. The Inland Revenue became concerned that many people, particularly in the IT industry, were working for one organisation for a long continuous period of time (that is, effectively as an employee) but were claiming to be self-employed (or working through their own limited companies) and thereby claiming any tax benefits that accrued. The Inland Revenue announced its intentions to address this abuse in what is now referred to as IR35 (the number of the Press Release in which it stated its intent). The purpose here is to alert readers to the issues that can arise – although it is unlikely that they would present problems in most research projects. If in doubt on any of these matters when entering into collaborative arrangements, readers should seek professional advice.

Returning to the more significant issues that arise when the research is undertaken by a consortium made up of various organisations (each of whom may themselves be employing staff) and self-employed contractors, the following employment related questions need to be addressed.

- Who is liable for any subsequent litigation that might arise as a result of actions by researchers working on the project?
- Who takes responsibility for the safety of those engaged on the research project?
- Is appropriate insurance cover in place?
- Who has ownership/copyright of the research instruments, data and reports prepared, gathered or written by each of the groups? (Copyright is the subject of Chapter 10.)
- Who has the right to disseminate (in any form) the findings from the research?

It is important that these issues are recognised at the outset and discussed between the parties (alongside the many other issues that will need to be resolved regarding the respective responsibilities of the different parties in undertaking the research). It is also good practice to ensure that the decisions are formally recorded and incorporated into any contract between the parties so that everyone has a clear understanding at the outset and any issues that arise during the course of the project or afterwards can be readily resolved.

So far the legal implications of the working relationship have been stressed. However, in arriving at an agreement all the parties would also wish to take full account of all ethical considerations. For example, while in law a self-employed person must take responsibility for their own safety, on ethical grounds, self-employed researchers on a project should be given the same advice and assistance as an employee. To take another example, while it is important to be clear about who can disseminate the findings of the research it is certainly not suggested that the contribution of all those who contributed to the research should not be appropriately recognised (which would be unethical). Ethical issues are discussed in Chapter 11. The significance of the contractual arrangement is to avoid misunderstanding and conflict, not to deny legitimate rights to anyone.

Contract research staff

A significant proportion of social researchers are engaged as contract research staff in higher education institutions. They are not established (tenured) academic employees of their institution but employed on a (usually short) fixed-term basis to work on a grant funded research project. The most detailed study of contract research staff (in all disciplines – not just social science) was conducted for the Scottish Higher Education Founding Council (SHEFC, 2001). The study set out to survey all contract research staff working in HE institutes in Scotland in 1998. By contacting respondents again in 2000, information was obtained on career progression as well as basic biographical information and their views and perceptions of being a contract researcher. The number of respondents from the social sciences and humanities was 214, but given the response rate of a little over 50 per cent, the number of contract research staff is nearer 400. Assuming there are ten times more contract researchers in England and Wales than in Scotland and others in Northern Ireland, it can be estimated that there are around 5,000 contract researchers in the social sciences and humanities at any one time. (And this does not take into account contract research staff who may be taking a career break for one reason or another.)

The position of the contract researcher is somewhat precarious; the pressure is continuously upon them to secure their next employment (around 40 per cent of respondents in the Scottish study were actively seeking their next post), leaving little time for considered career development. While the funding body would meet the costs of the basic salary, the perception (and the reality in many cases) was that the employing institution did not appreciate fully the contribution contract staff made to either the growth of knowledge or to the life of the institution and little was done to further the careers of contract researchers. As a consequence morale was low amongst contract staff.

Concerns regarding the plight of contract research staff (across all disciplines) and the need for more effective career management surfaced in the Government White Paper of 1993 *Realising Our Potential*. The White Paper tasked the research councils to work with higher education institutions with two objectives in mind:

1 More effective career management and development of contract research staff by the higher education institutions
2 Grant-making arrangements of the research councils should help HEIs discharge those responsibilities, and the council should look at the scope to put greater emphasis on longer-term or more personal forms of research support.

In 1995 a House of Lords Select Committee hearing examined issues relating to contract research staff and recommended that:

- contract staff should have the same status and rights as established colleagues of equivalent rank
- universities should have sound policies for the management of contract staff
- universities should improve counselling, career advice and retraining for contract staff
- universities should earmark funds to bridge gaps between contracts for contract staff
- universities should create longer-term fellowships for the most able scientists
- universities should pay attention to the need for students to be educated through science to careers which may be unrelated to academia
- better advice should be provided to students regarding careers and university career services should serve contract staff as well as undergraduates.

A Concordat to Provide a Framework for the Career Management of Contract Research Staff in Universities and Colleges

The bodies representing Vice-Chancellors and Principals of HE institutions in the UK and the research councils together with the British Academy and the Royal Society responded to the White Paper by agreeing in 1996 to adopt *A Concordat to Provide a Framework for the Career Management of Contract Research Staff in Universities and Colleges* (www.universitiesuk.ac.uk/activities/RCIdown loads/rciconcordat.pdf).

The parties to the Concordat agreed that the framework for the more effective career management of the contract research staff should be based on the following principles:

- promoting the active personnel and career management of contract researchers, recognising the important contribution they make to the success of their employing institutions, including the dissemination of research results and new techniques
- acceptance by the universities and colleges of the importance of regular review and career guidance for contract researchers, to ensure that they receive appropriate and timely advice, support, and encouragement to develop their careers and to take responsibility for so doing
- an understanding between the funding bodies and the universities and colleges of their respective roles and responsibilities: (a) in meeting the costs associated with management of these staff, including career guidance and retraining or other appropriate arrangements to realise broader career opportunities upon the expiry of the contract researcher's fixed-term appointment; (b) in keeping under review funding levels for personal or longer-term forms of support in academic research.

Determining the detailed personnel and career management arrangements for contract research staff was seen as the responsibility of the universities and colleges as the employers. But the funding bodies would wish to be satisfied, as a key condition of providing grants and fellowships to the universities and colleges, that those institutions have in place and apply effective career management policies. The Concordat set standards of personnel management.

1   *recruitment*, so that the opportunities provided by contract research posts are, as far as possible known and used:

   •   to provide research training and continuing development for researchers at an early stage of a research career, which may subsequently be pursued in academia, industry, commerce, or the wider public sector; or

   •   for the planned career development of existing contract staff, again with the possibility of that development subsequently taking place in academia, industry, commerce, or the wider public sector; or

   •   as 're-entry' routes for researchers who have taken time out from their careers.

2   *performance management arrangements*, to ensure that research supervisors provide effective research environments for the training and development of researchers. In addition, there should be in place systems of:

   •   *supervision*, in order that contract researchers gain the maximum benefit from the training and development opportunities provided by the research environment in which they work

   •   *regular review*, enabling the contract researcher and his or her supervisor – and ultimately the university or college as the employer – to form the best possible assessment of, and feedback on, the individual's potential, whether for a research career in academia, industry, commerce, the wider public sector or in some other direction.

3   *rewards and other terms and conditions of service for contract research staff (for example, rates of pay, provisions for leave and sick leave, pensions, access to facilities)* which are in line with those for established staff, thus avoiding the tendency for contract researchers to feel isolated from, and disadvantaged in relation to, those groups of employees. A key element is an assurance of *equal opportunities* and the elimination of practices linked to the short-term nature of contracts which indirectly discriminate against women. Maternity leave and pay provisions for contract staff should be in line with the provisions for established staff, subject to the fixed-term period of the employment contract;

4   *in-service training* in the form of appropriate specialist or general training. Demonstrating and teaching duties should be encouraged within the limits set by grant conditions;

5   *career guidance and development*, for example to inform decisions by contract research staff on a change of career direction if the opportunities are limited

or if they do not wish to remain in research or are not suited to such a career, and encouragement of talented researchers with advice on opportunities inside and outside the employing institution.

The Concordat also placed an obligation on funding bodies to amend the terms of their contracts where necessary to meet the costs of these enhanced conditions of service.

The Research Careers Initiative

The Office of Science and Technology facilitated the establishment in 1997 of the Research Careers Initiative, with representation from the higher education funding councils, the research councils, the charities, the universities and the university staff unions. The Research Careers Initiative was chaired by Professor Sir Gareth Roberts, its remit being to monitor the implementation of the Concordat and to identify, encourage and disseminate best practice. The RCI had three original objectives:

1   changing the culture in which contract research staff worked so that they were seen as central to the pursuit of good science research
2   to provide them with a viable career structure
3   to secure adjustments to national funding systems so that change could be enabled.

After the Concordat was adopted, university employers and funding agencies agreed standards, expectations and responsibilities for the proper management and career development of contract research staff. *The Research Careers Initiative Final Report 1997–2002* (www.universitiesuk.ac.uk/activities/RCIdownloads/RCI_final.pdf) records that national and institutional policies for research staff are stronger and clearer. Good practice in such areas as staff appraisal, in-service training and career guidance has been implemented. However, it noted that more needed to be done in terms of greater security of employment (and for staff to be treated as an integral part of the institutions in which they work). Greater clarity of career paths has still to be achieved and steps are needed to ensure that women and minority groups are not disproportionately disadvantaged through being employed on short-term contracts.

Other developments have occurred during the period of the RCI or since its conclusion. An important external development has been the introduction of the Europe-wide Fixed-Term Regulations, which came into force in October 2002. These regulations will have a major impact on research careers by improving employment rights and giving access to compensation for redundancy. Following the Regulations, staff can only be employed on a fixed-term contract if the contract is tied to a specific grant, is to cover maternity leave, long-term sickness or is for less than twelve weeks. Otherwise the person is considered permanently employed. After two years a person is entitled to redundancy payment even if during that period he or she was employed on a fixed-term contract.

In a separate initiative, the government has provided an additional £100 million a year to raise the salaries of researchers and to improve training opportunities. To ensure compliance, the research councils are placing greater emphasis on an institution's performance in the management of contract researchers when granting funding. The number of fellowships available to researchers at different stages of their career has greatly increased. (Fellowships as a form of funding social research are discussed in Chapter 4.)

Most recently, the government is changing the fundamental structure for funding research. The current dual funding system (whereby the research councils fund the direct costs and pay an 'institutional overhead' from which the host institution meets the cost of providing infrastructure and any costs of employing research staff other than direct salary costs) is to be phased out. The future direction is to move towards the research councils meeting the full economic costs of research. Under such an arrangement, institutions will be able to incorporate in grant applications an element to cover the costs of training and the career development of contract research staff.

The ESRC is expanding training and career development. Support at present is skewed towards early post-doctoral careers, so future initiatives will be targeted at the needs of researchers at 'mid-career'. Finally, the ESRC has adopted 'capacity' as one of its priority themes. In essence this means that the council will explicitly address the need to grow and develop the number and quality of social researchers in the UK. Initiatives will follow under this priority theme to enhance the important role contract research staff play in social research in this country.

Safety of researchers

In his book on the dangers social researchers face, Lee (1995) points out that much of the subject matter of social research involves violence, conflict, sensitive or deviant behaviour of one sort or another involving contact with the perpetrators or victims of that behaviour. However, citing reviews of their work, Lee also points out that the greatest dangers an anthropologist faces in the course of his or her research are falls, road accidents and disease (in particular malaria and hepatitis). Harm is not just physical, it can be psychological such as trauma and stress resulting from the sensitive nature of the research, fear, harassment or simply overwork. Researchers also face risks of false and malicious accusations of improper conduct and litigation as a result of such allegations. Litigation may also follow allegations of libel or breaches of confidentiality. Stigmatisation and perhaps even prosecution may follow in the wake of research on certain topics, however professionally, objectively or impartially that research was conducted. Personally, I would not undertake research on internet child pornography, however important the issue or how responsible and respectable the sponsor. The risks to my reputation, I consider to be too great.

Safety thus takes many forms and risks can arise from routine activities (similar to those faced by many other groups of workers) as well as risks which can be seen as particular to social research or specific to any one project. All risks need to be considered and preventive action taken.

A method of proceeding is to undertake a risk analysis along the lines described in Chapter 2. Risks need to be identified and strategies devised for minimising or dealing with those risks. The next steps are to timetable when action needs to be taken and designate who is to take responsibility for the action.

Although we are dealing here with specific dangers to individuals, it is important to be aware that any dangers to individuals and strategies for dealing with them can impact on the design, quality and cost of the project. Safety, and its implications, should be thought through at the design and planning stage of the project, even if all the actions cannot be implemented immediately. Furthermore, identification of potential dangers may influence decisions on the type of person to be recruited to the team to undertake specific tasks. A few examples will serve to illustrate these points.

Face to face interviews with certain research subjects may pose particular risks but to substitute postal questionnaires or telephone interviews may compromise the quality, and hence the value, of the research. The research subjects may be even more difficult to reach by phone or may have difficulties with literacy, deterring them from completing a written questionnaire. For whatever reason, the response rate is likely to be lower and the quality of the data reduced if the alternative research designs are adopted. Having considered the detrimental effects to the study arising from the alternatives, on balance a face-to-face interview may be required. The issue then is to minimise the risks to the safety of the researchers, perhaps by paying for respondents to travel to a safe venue or for an escort to accompany the interviewer. But either will add to the costs of the project.

A risk that all workers face, not just social researchers, is theft (most likely from their car or from their person) of their equipment; briefcase, laptop, mobile phone, tape recorder, etc. As well as the distress and inconvenience caused to the individual researcher and the financial value of the items stolen, the loss may also be of vital and irreplaceable information to the research project, such as contact numbers and addresses, completed questionnaires and recordings of interviews. Much of the information stolen may be confidential. Hence strategies need to be devised to minimise the risk of the event occurring but also to minimise the consequences to the project should the event occur. Such preventative measures could include duplicating information, emailing electronic data to the research institution immediately it has been collected and separating the tapes from the tape recorder. In order to preserve confidentiality, identifiers could be separated from the data and separate records kept of how the two relate.

Lee (1995) provides many examples of the difficulties faced by ethnographic researchers and the situations in which they may find themselves. Researchers may be viewed with suspicion, at least initially, and by their actions may be required to prove their trustworthiness. Researchers will need to consider how they present themselves and their research and how they propose to ensure confidentiality to their research subjects. Who funds the project may be a particular matter of concern in either raising or allaying suspicions.

Certain situations may require a researcher with particular characteristics, attributes or level and type of previous experience. The research topic may prompt considerations of the researcher's gender, age, ethnicity and cultural background, including fluency in languages other than English. The initial stakeholder analysis and prior contact with research subjects may help clarify and resolve these issues. Bear in mind that safety is but one concern here. These issues also need to be addressed from the perspectives of methodology and quality and all three should be considered at the same time – at the design and planning stage of the project.

Guides and sources of information

A good deal of useful, practical advice on how to protect staff and minimise risks to personal safety is now readily available. First the research manager will need to be familiar with health and safety protocols and procedures within his or her organisation. All organisations are required by law to address health and safety and someone within the organisation will be designated as responsible for these matters, and in large organisations there will exist a network of departmental health and safety officers. These designated officers can be consulted and they should be aware of basic training courses run by or for the organisation. Do not regard in-house training as being only relevant to working within the organisation. Basic courses on lifting, posture and using IT equipment also have relevance to field research, in particular travelling and conducting interviews.

The Suzy Lamplugh Trust is a source of much valuable information (www.suzylamplugh.org/home/index.shtml). Suzy Lamplugh was a 25-year-old estate agent who went to meet an unknown client in 1986 and has never been seen since. Suzy's mother Diana set up a trust in that year in her daughter's name devoted to highlighting 'the risks people face and to offer advice, action and support to minimise those risks' (Suzy Lamplugh Trust website).

The Trust has produced many reasonably priced detailed practical guides, *Personal Safety at Work* perhaps being the most relevant to social researchers. The Trust also offers consultancy advice, training and has a shop selling equipment, such as personal alarms.

The Social Research Association has recently produced *A Code of Practice for the Safety of Social Researchers*, which is available free at its website, www.the-sra.org.uk. The guide sets out clearly the issues which need to be thought through but provides less detailed practical advice on some aspects of personal safety than the Suzy Lamplugh Trust document.

Survey organisations, such as the Office for National Statistics, the National Centre for Social Research and all commercial market research companies with a large field force of interviewers, will have produced guidance on personal safety and will have considerable experience to pass on. The Market Research Society has published *Health and Safety Guidelines for Face to Face Interviewers*, which is available free at its website (www.marketresearch.org.uk/standards/downloads/drafths.pdf).

Further advice can been sought from local organisations, local officials and groups. If the research is to be carried out in institutions (for example, schools or hospitals) the employees of those institutions will be a source of advice. They can be consulted on safety matters as part of the stakeholder analysis. If the research is to be based in a particular geographical location, the police or local community leaders will have valuable advice to offer (and it may be worth informing the police of the research in any case). A prior visit to the location may also yield important information.

The risks associated with undertaking research in other countries and health risks are not well covered in the guides described above. Risks to health may be heightened because the research involves contacts with infected groups (such as drug misusers) or based in institutions where disease is more prevalent. Doctors or other health officials should be contacted on appropriate conduct and on any precautionary measures that should be taken, such as injections. Avoid coming into close contact with the interviewee or sharing cups or drinks. Even sharing pens can transmit infection.

Research in certain parts of the world entails greater health risks. A good source of information here is the Foreign and Commonwealth Office website (www. fco.gov.uk). On its home page under the section 'Services' an option is *Travel Advice by Country*. For each country of the world information is given on terrorism, crime, the political situation, road and rail safety and health (as well as other advice on documents required, contact details of the local Embassy, etc.). In the section on health, links are provided to the Department of Health website which contains information on the diseases prevalent in the country and the inoculations required or recommended.

More prosaically, backache and headache, wrist, neck and eye strain may result from bad posture and poor lighting. These concerns should be addressed by the research organisation's health and safety officer.

Stress

A commitment to health and safety extends to tackling work-related stress. It is an employer's duty in law to ensure that employees are not made ill by their work. Stress is defined as the adverse reaction people have to excessive pressure; it is not itself a disease but it can lead to mental and physical ill-health. Because stress can affect people in different ways its symptoms and manifestations can vary. To detect stress, look out for mood swings and irritability. Physical symptoms can include frequent headaches, stomach disorders, tiredness, weight loss and coughs and colds brought about by low immunity. Stress is also likely to affect a person's performance at work and be apparent from a reduced quality of their work, indecision and increased absenteeism. People suffering from stress may also drink and smoke more and even resort to taking drugs.

Stress at work is not simply caused by overwork, although the demands of the job are often a major contributory factor. Lack of support, lack of control, the culture of the organisation and relationships with colleagues, bullying or harassment can all take their toll. Some of these are preventable by ensuring a supportive environment and sympathetic management. (See Chapter 8 where team building and issues about managing, leading and motivating people are discussed.) Other factors, for example harassment, cannot always be effectively prevented in advance but will require swift remedial action should it occur. Of course, not all stress is work-related. It may stem from financial or domestic difficulties and in these circumstances the manager and other work colleagues will have less power to deal with the cause.

Stress suffered by others is most often discussed, but what about the project manager's own stress? Do not ignore your own symptoms. Apart from being concerned about your own well-being, your stress could have adverse affects on others and for the smooth running of the project. The research manager has a duty to others to manage his/her own stress. Think what might be causing the stress and take remedial action. If it is outside your control to affect change, consult with those who do have the power. If you cannot isolate the cause seek help.

Further information on stress is available at the Health and Safety Executive website. Their publication *Work-related Stress: A short guide* has useful tips on 'what managers can do' to reduce stress occurring. It can be obtained from www.hse.gov.uk/pubns/indg281.pdf.

Budgeting for safety

Ensuring safety may well incur costs (as a result of changes to the methodology, purchasing specialist equipment, additional travel and subsistence or training). These costs should be itemised, estimated and budgeted for in the initial application. However, clarity may be needed on whether the funder or the employer should bear the cost. Does the additional cost arise specifically as a result of the project (which the funder should meet) or can it be regarded as part of the employer's general responsibility for the welfare of their employees (which the employer should meet)? A discussion with the funding body may be necessary.

Finally, while risks need to be anticipated and minimised, attention also needs to be given to appropriate action should the event occur. The research manager should check that all appropriate insurance is in place to cover eventualities, that support is in place for any team member who needs it and that action can be taken to recover any damage to the project.

8 Implementing the project

Project management texts imply that there is a clear distinction between each phase of a project, that a project progresses distinctively from one phase to another and that the tasks in each phase are clearly defined. This has not always been my experience of social research projects, where it has not always been clear when one moves from planning to implementation. Obviously there is a point where the proposal to do the work becomes a reality, a knowledge that the project will go ahead. The watershed is often a letter from the funding or commissioning body stating that the application or tender has been successful. But, depending on the project and the people involved, further negotiations may be needed to iron out details before the contract can be signed. Staff may need to be recruited, appointments being dependent on securing funding. On the other hand, the team who will be working on the project may already be employed by the organisation who developed the original proposal. They may be already working as a team completing an existing project.

Nevertheless, whatever remains to be clarified at the beginning, the project will comprise dedicated research staff assembled to work on the project, agreed aims and objectives, a plan, a budget and a timescale. The project will also have a customer, who may be the sponsor of the research or the team itself if they initiated the research and applied for a grant to conduct the project. In addition to the customers, there is likely to be a range of different stakeholders.

At the implementation stage, the project manager/principal investigator will have four interrelated responsibilities:

- to report periodically to the sponsor and/or a Steering Committee that has been convened
- to manage the team
- to monitor, control and direct the project in order to keep it on track and within budget
- to ensure that the work is being undertaken to the required quality standard.

Each is considered in this chapter.

Liaison with the sponsor

It is important to have clear lines of communication with the commissioning or sponsoring body and it is in the interest of all concerned that this type of contact exists. Regular contact will allow the project to remain on course even if sponsors' interests change focus during the project. I much prefer to have someone within the commissioning organisation designated as the point of contact with my project. Ideally that person should also have delegated authority on behalf of the commissioning organisation to suggest and agree to small changes to the project (even if they have to consult with others within the organisation beforehand). What often happens during the course of the project is the need to make small amendments relatively quickly; for example, one school or prison wishes to withdraw from the study because it is having an inspection, or is being refurbished, and a substitute is required.

It is good practice to stay in regular contact with the designated contact person, and to involve them in the project by inviting them to the occasional project meeting, to seek their comments on any draft research instruments, to 'sit in' on briefing meetings prior to fieldwork and even to spend a day in the field. In addition to the advice they may offer, they will gain first-hand experience of the strengths and limitations of the information collected. Those insights will put them in a better position to judge the outputs from the project and the conclusions that can be drawn from it.

Steering Committee

In addition to a dedicated contact person, the sponsor may set up a Steering Committee. Such a committee is typically made up of the lead policy customer for the research, usually a relatively senior person within the sponsoring organisation (who is often the Chair) and representatives from other policy departments within the organisation who also have an interest in the subject area. The contact person from the sponsoring organisation, as the contract manager, will also be a member and may be the Secretary to the committee. Representatives of practitioner groups or other major stakeholders will also join the committee (for example, a representative of the teaching profession, local authority associations, the police and so on, depending on the project). If the focus of the project is to evaluate a specific programme or intervention, representatives of the agency or group running the programme will be members. One or two outside experts, perhaps academics, might be asked to join in view of their special knowledge of the subject or familiarity with the methodology. The research team undertaking the project will, of course, also be on the Steering Committee. Committees can thus vary in size and it is not uncommon to find a dozen people attending the meetings, although keeping membership to below eight helps the committee to function, especially when taking decisions.

The purpose of the Steering Committee is, as the term implies, to guide the project and to take any major decisions that may affect the project. It will periodically receive and consider progress reports from the project team. It can agree to changes in focus, methodology and often to the budget. The executive power of the Steering Committee to instigate changes to the project separates it from an Advisory Committee, which exists purely to give advice to the team but has no say (other than by persuasion) on how the project should be run and certainly has no control over resources.

Steering Committees meet regularly throughout the project, quarterly, every six months or at key points within the project cycle, perhaps at or near milestones. A purpose may be to guide the next stage or to approve a previous stage and agree payment.

Many project managers have a less than favourable opinion of Steering Committees. This view is reinforced by their generally negative experience of Steering Committees, judging them to be of little constructive value. If large and unwieldy, comprising members having little interest or commitment to the project, their value is limited, even counter productive. It is often difficult to find a mutually convenient date for all the members, so the meeting either goes ahead with many members not attending (more junior staff attending in their place who have little knowledge of the project and nothing useful to contribute) or the meeting is put back to a later date and after the point when its decisions are needed. Preparing for, and attending Steering Committee meetings, can be very time-consuming and if nothing positive comes out of the meeting that time is wasted. It is thus good practice to schedule dates of all Steering Committee meetings at the beginning of the project as this helps to avoid postponements and delays.

However, as a project manager, I find Steering Committees can be useful and, on balance, I would prefer to have one. Steering Committees often serve as a useful forum for stakeholders, forcing them, however half-heartedly, to periodically engage with the project. Steering Group meetings can be an opportunity to negotiate access and obtain advice and information and, importantly, to air any ethical issues that may arise. Although minor changes may have been agreed with the contact person, a Steering Committee meeting is the opportunity to endorse and record those decisions. In addition, the discipline of formally reporting progress and emerging findings to a Steering Committee can smooth the path of the final report.

Managing the team

At the earliest opportunity a start-up meeting should be convened at which the team should be fully briefed on the project and each member on their respective responsibilities. The team could comprise researchers from the same organisation or researchers from different organisations if the project is to be undertaken by a consortium. The project proposal, the project plan and the responsibility chart that have been prepared should be circulated prior to the meeting. At the meeting everyone should be encouraged to contribute by making their views known and by asking questions to seek clarification, particularly of their own roles and responsibilities. The meeting will also serve to encourage the team to take collective ownership of the project.

Some researchers may be new to the project and perhaps even new to the organisation if they were recruited from outside. New staff will need special consideration and encouragement to participate at start-up meetings. I strongly believe that the project manager and other senior members of the team should make every effort to induct new staff into the organisation and to take time to brief them on the project and the part they are to play. By making this effort, the project manager will be seen to be committed to the project and supportive of those engaged on it, thereby gaining the respect and confidence of the new team member. By becoming involved the project manager will also appear approachable and sensitive to staff concerns. Not to make this effort at the outset will lead to negative feelings that will probably never be fully eradicated. In reality, however, the project manager will have many other duties to attend to and cannot be expected to be available at all times. Consider appointing one of the team to act as mentor to any new member of staff, who can be on hand to help with those mundane but essential tasks, such as finding the way around the campus or the building, registering with the library, etc.

Job satisfaction and motivation

Teams are more effective and productive if members are enthusiastic and have a positive attitude throughout the project. A variety of factors contribute to making a researcher feel worthwhile, satisfied and highly motivated in their work, such as:

- they feel that the work generally is demanding, challenging and intellectually stimulating (accepting that some elements will be mundane and repetitive) but that the level of work is not unrealistic and overburdening
- they feel that their effort is being recognised, appreciated and rewarded appropriately
- they have a degree of responsibility, autonomy and control and that they are consulted over their component of the project
- they are treated fairly as professionals and their views respected
- that the work is contributing to their personal and professional development.

Note the absence from this list of money and promotion. Obviously both motivate team members and are likely to arise at some point if a person stays a period of time within an organisation, but they are unlikely to be issues during the life cycle of the specific project (unless a more senior person leaves the project part way through creating an unexpected vacancy). Researchers will be aware of the post and the salary attached to it when applying for the job. Furthermore, pay and promotion will, in most cases, be outside the control of the project manager, and team members will know this. What will be of more immediate concern to researchers is that the project provides an opportunity to develop their skills, competencies and experiences which will put them in a position to apply for more senior posts after the project has concluded or at a later point in their careers.

Management and leadership

It is the manager's responsibility to devise and implement practices and procedures and a culture that produces efficient and effective team-working whilst enabling individual team members to flourish. Taking into account the factors that motivate staff, the project manager needs to develop a culture, which encourages:

- respect and fairness
- openness and honesty
- two-way communication and the exchange of information
- ideas, innovations and suggestions
- participation and involvement in decision-making
- mutual support.

Although all team members should be involved in discussions where appropriate, at the end of the day it is the manager's responsibility to lead and direct. Having consulted and weighed all other relevant information, a good manager should give clear and unambiguous directions on how to progress the work. The manager's job is also to ensure that the research reaches the quality standards agreed in the proposal.

The qualities of a good project manager/team leader, are, I believe:

- making time for the project and for dealing with the concerns of team members
- being fully committed and interested
- being fully informed of the project, and hence in a position to control events
- having analytical and good problem-solving skills
- being involved in the tough decisions and taking responsibility for implementing them (usually a 'tricky' negotiation with a stakeholder)
- having good influencing and communication skills
- being sincere, honest and open
- having professional skills and experience
- ready to role up his/her sleeves to help out when demands require.

For me 'actions speak louder than words' and I find commitment, hard work and professional skills are inspirational. Leading by example is the best way to earn the respect of the team. Team members can soon see through falsehood and insincerity and become resentful if they feel the leader is not pulling his/her weight.

One trap to avoid as project manager/leader is to assume that you are just one of the team or to act as an equal to other team members. The project manager is not, and cannot be, as he/she has more information, more knowledge and more power than other team members and it is his/her responsibility to use the information, knowledge and power wisely. The difference in position does not in any way preclude the project manager from being approachable, sharing interests or mixing socially with other team members, but in the context of the project, the difference remains.

A good project manager/leader should:

Delegate to team members authority and responsibility for tasks where possible. But before doing so, make sure that the person understands the task, is properly skilled and equipped to carry out the task successfully and that he/she has the time and resources to complete it. Furthermore, arrange to monitor progress so that additional support or remedial action can be taken to ensure the job gets done.

Give constructive feedback on performance Praise work well done and always make positive comments before being critical. Try to be constructive when correcting poor performance. Do not leave feedback until the task has been completed but offer comments and judgements as the work is progressing. People like to know that they are 'on the right track' and 'doing a good job'. Leaving feedback to the end provokes the response 'if he/she didn't want me to do it that way they should have said before, not left it 'til now to tell me'.

Encourage and promote staff development Specific instruction, guidance and training may be required for the immediate tasks to hand, but over and above that team members should be encouraged to formulate a career development plan, setting out how their own personal skills and competencies might be developed. Researchers should not simply seek to improve their expertise in research methods, but should take opportunities to develop competencies in management, negotiation and, especially, communication.

Managers can help develop that plan and ensure that it is put into practice by making time and money available to attend external training courses. Much can be achieved within the project itself by arranging joint working such that team members learn from each other. So far as it is practicable, junior staff should attend external meetings and participate in presentations and in preparing reports. The Concordat relating to the employment of contract research staff (discussed in Chapter 7) recognises the importance of staff development and commits employers to establishing career development programmes.

Guidelines established by government departments recommend that government social researchers should expect to receive ten to twelve days training annually. Career development plans should feature prominently in any formal staff appraisal system in operation within the organisation, but every opportunity should be taken to discuss training and development more frequently and less formally.

Finally, the project manager also needs to think of his/her own training needs – all professionals must invest in life-long learning. Training in how to deal with the media in order that the results of the research reach a wider audience may be needed.

Managing your boss

It is not just junior staff that need managing, but bosses, too, as a good working relationship with one's boss is imperative. Put yourself in your manager's position and try to understand his/her objectives, values, priorities, pressures and constraints. In other words, try and appreciate how the project appears from your boss' perspective. Show empathy with your manager's situation and find ways of supporting or compensating for the weaker aspects of his/her style. Avoid direct confrontation and attempts to undermine your boss' position, but do not be too passive or ignore problems. Discuss problems, but always with a view to arriving at a constructive and mutually agreed solution.

Time management

Effective project management requires *time*. Make sure that sufficient time has been allocated in the project proposal to undertake the task properly. Project management need not be a full-time occupation, other activities can be pursued alongside (such as teaching, administration or indeed work on different projects), but these other activities should never be allowed to consume the time that has been allocated to the project. Similar comments apply to those working on the project, who also need to manage their time well. They too may be only part-time on the project and juggling their own time between various activities. It is my experience that when time is pressing, the project is often the first to suffer, especially project management. (Usually because the project manager is the most likely to experience competing pressures and, at the time, project management appears the least urgent activity – but that does not make it least important.)

If research is to be combined with other activities make as clear a distinction between activities as possible, in terms of time, location and organisational structure. Block out time such that it is clear that certain days are for one activity, other days for another. If different activities can be undertaken at different locations this will minimise interruptions. Organisational separation will also minimise being expected to deal with other unrelated tasks ('while you're here could you also. . . . '). Of course, it is not always realistic to be able to make such clear separations between activities. Even so, at least think through how the different activities may impact on each other and how that might best be managed.

So far, the time a person is on or off the project has been considered. But time working on the project also has to be managed in order that it is used to best effect. Classic time management states that one should first analyse how time is spent on different tasks. To facilitate this, one has to keep a record of time spent on different activities. At this point people shy away, imaging the imposition of detailed time-recording systems. I have sympathy with this, they tend to serve no useful purpose as the information is sent off somewhere in the organisation and no use is made of it. Many time-recording systems have a tendency to become an end in themselves and a very time-consuming and stressful activity for those involved. However, they need not be, and a broad record of how time is spent can be very informative and helpful. All I need is a second diary in which I record time spent on different tasks. My entries are rarely detailed, often only one line 'teaching at university', 'Steering Group meeting for project xxx'. Sometimes two entries may be required: 'a.m. project xxx team meeting; p.m. analysing yyy data'. On occasion more entries are required. Not only does the information assist me in assessing whether my time is being put to best use, but it also enables me to monitor whether the project is running according to plan. (Monitoring is discussed later in this chapter.)

Prioritise work according to what is important and what is urgent. Ask what needs to be done, do the important. Also ask what *ought* to be delegated to others. (Management texts say what *can* be delegated, implying that the manager should not do anything someone else can do or has carte blanche to dump anything on anyone else regardless of the other person's workload. Good leadership, as well as keeping the project on track, may require the project manager to step in and take on some tasks even if others could do them.)

Do not just think and plan your own time, think of the impact on others of what you do. Do not waste other people's time.

Plan to use time by drawing up lists of what is to be done each day or by a certain point and make sure it is achieved. 'Worst first' – do not put off the unpleasant or the more demanding; get them out of the way early on.

Keep your workspace clear and uncluttered. Handle each piece of paper once only – do not keep starting jobs and putting them down to be returned to later. If the paper requires action then act. If it does not require any action on your part, either pass it on to the person who needs to see it, file it or throw it away.

Block out certain periods of the day for certain activities, such as reading the post or emails. Two periods a day should be sufficient, any more is disruptive (and probably a sign that you are finding an excuse not to do something that needs doing). Avoid continual phone interruptions. Divert calls to an answerphone for certain periods of the day and while you are engaged on a specific task. Make phone calls in batches rather than individually.

Take charge of your workload and learn to say no. When being dumped upon, explain your situation and explain what can and cannot be done as a consequence of the additional tasks. Saying nothing until you have to explain it is all going to be late will appear as excuses to cover up incompetence.

Monitoring, controlling and directing

Monitoring, controlling and directing are the central and predominant activities of the implementation stage and the main task of the project manager/principal investigator. In order to direct and control, progress has to be monitored. If you don't know where you are you will not know how to get to where you want to be. Optimism characterises the early stages of the project, but as the project progresses aspects that were regarded as challenges now become problems. Catastrophic events, such as access not being granted or data that was expected not being available, are easily recognised. What is more typical, and often more invasive, is day-by-day slippage, which being small is ignored, but has a habit of accumulating and becoming a significant delay. Close monitoring will alert the project manager to 'drift' and indicate whether corrective action is needed.

What needs to be monitored?

1   progress of the project
2   quality of the work
3   spend against budget
4   staff performance and development
5   health and safety of staff
6   risks to the project
7   sponsor's and other stakeholders' interest and involvement
8   dissemination.

All would agree that points 1 to 3 need to be monitored, but I would add points 4 to 8 too. Throughout this book I have emphasised that all aspects of a project need to be kept under constant review as circumstances can change throughout the project life cycle. Considering each in turn:

Progress of the project

A close check is needed on whether the work is progressing to schedule and whether individual components are starting and finishing at the pre-specified time. (This is discussed further, later in this section.)

Quality of work

Quality is also discussed later in this chapter where the point is forcibly made that monitoring is needed to ensure standards are being met.

Spend against budget

In most organisations systems will be in place to handle project budgets, the central finance department will invoice the funding body and standard forms and procedures will be in place to buy equipment, submit expenses, etc. Staff will receive salaries through the organisations' payroll systems. The project will most likely be assigned a project code number against which all payments will be registered. However, with the exception of staff salaries, it will invariably be the project manager's task to initiate action or authorise expenditure and incidental payments.

It is imperative, therefore, that the project manager becomes fully acquainted and knowledgeable of the systems in operation. He/she will also need to link that system to the budget profile of the project. For example, if payment is based on reaching a milestone, the project manager will need to know that the milestone has been reached, that it triggers an invoice and whoever is to submit the invoice is notified.

Monitoring is also a prerequisite for controlling the budget. You cannot control costs if the money has already been spent. Being able to reallocate funds from one project sub-head to another (a virement), is often an important mechanism for redirecting the project and bringing it back on track; for example, making savings on photocopying and telephone calls to pay for the increased costs of transcriptions of taped interviews.

The project manager will also be expected to reconcile financial errors should they occur. (And they usually come to light late in the project when much of the information has long since disappeared into an administrative system thereby being virtually impossible to retrieve.) Reconciling anomalies is at best time-consuming and at worst impossible. From my experience the problems arise because the systems in large organisations tend to involve too many steps and stages with different individuals responsible at each stage. Tasks finish up falling between two stools. On one project I found that £3,000 of expenses had not been claimed from the funding body because everyone thought it was someone else's responsibility to submit the claim.

In an attempt to minimise problems, I like to keep close control of the budget. I make it a rule that expense claim forms and all receipts for equipment come via me and are not sent direct to the finance section. I have a copy taken which is then filed so that I have a complete record of expenditure. I also monitor staff costs. Payroll is relatively straightforward, but increasingly individuals are being costed to a project or charged out at a daily rate to work on the project for a certain number of days. I need to know how many days they have worked on the project and how much this has cost the project. (Information on time and cost is then set alongside information on what has been done and what has still to be done in order to gauge whether the work is on track or whether remedial action is necessary.)

Many project managers find financial budgeting irksome or difficult, often, I think, as a result of giving insufficient attention to it. In practice, if simple procedures are adopted, comprehensive records kept and a little, but regular, attention given to it, monitoring the budget should not prove burdensome. In a larger research centre with many projects running, assistance will be required and it is important to have one person with appropriate skills dedicated to collating all financial information and monitoring the budget. However, as a Director of that Centre I would still keep a close eye on budgets and establish an effective working relationship with the dedicated finance officer.

Staff performance and development

Check that team members are implementing their personal development plan. Take action to ensure that everyone is taking opportunities within the project to gain knowledge and experience. Identify appropriate training courses for team members and adapt work schedules so that they can attend.

Health and safety of staff

The best possible health and safety audit should have been undertaken at the outset. However, once the project is underway, especially the fieldwork stage, experience can be drawn upon to reassess risks and amend any preventive action that has been implemented.

Of equal importance is to monitor the hours staff are working and how they are coping with the demands and pressures of the work. Are any of the team showing signs of stress and what actions can be taken to alleviate the problem? Health and safety was discussed in Chapter 7.

Risks to the project

A risk analysis will have been undertaken when preparing the initial proposal but it will require periodic review. As discussed in Chapter 2 the profile of risks changes and alters during the course of a project so needs to be monitored constantly.

Sponsor's and other stakeholders' interest and involvement

If contracted to a sponsor, it is essential to keep abreast of any shift in policy focus. Negotiations with stakeholders will be ongoing throughout the project, and these will have been anticipated in the proposal and, in many cases, will have begun before the project formally started. But stakeholders will change during the course of a project as individuals move on in their careers and are replaced. The relative importance of a stakeholder may also change and stakeholders may change their attitude towards the project. Relationships with stakeholders can never be taken for granted.

Dissemination

A dissemination strategy will have been formulated as part of the proposal and Chapter 9 emphasises the importance of beginning the task of writing reports early in the project life cycle. Monitoring is required to assess whether the strategy is being pursued and to establish what progress is being made on the reports and other outputs.

How to monitor

Information on how the project is progressing can be obtained in a variety of ways, from:

- inspection
- audit
- testing
- observation
- discussion with individuals
- group meetings
- written reports.

All methods have their strengths and should be adopted. Over-reliance on just one method is not advisable. A colleague of mine learnt this lesson the hard way. On one project he regularly asked the researcher how the project he was working on was progressing. Every time the response was 'okay'. But when the assistant left the project part way through, my colleague found that matters were far from okay. Little had been done. By not obtaining other information he had no means of corroborating or challenging the impression given by the researcher.

Of course, inspection, auditing and testing of one's work can appear threatening to the social researcher. Even observation, discussion, meetings and comments on written reports can feel uncomfortable. The challenge to management is to implement these methods of obtaining the required information in a way that does not undermine the autonomy or the self-esteem of the members of the team. As managers of social research projects we tend not to use the terms inspection, auditing and testing but talk instead of sharing, advising or piloting. If a culture is established which promotes openness and the project manager appears interested, approachable and supportive rather than autocratic and judgemental, team members will engage, share information and not conceal problems.

Monitoring should not be too bureaucratic and certainly not overburdening. It takes time to attend meetings and write progress reports. Think of the opportunity costs of such activities; they will divert time that could otherwise be spent on the project.

Meetings can take one of several formats.

One-to-one meetings between the project manager and an individual team member —
arranged to discuss the individual's particular component of the project, their concerns and their contribution to the project.

Internal project meetings – to enable all members of the team to hear how parts other than their own are progressing and to air and resolve issues that affect more than one component of the project or team member. (Internal project meetings also serve to reinforce the recognition that the project is a team effort.)

External (often Steering Group) meetings with stakeholders – arranged to report progress to funders, to communicate emerging findings, to negotiate access, to obtain advice or agreement.

Of whatever type, meetings should only be convened if necessary to serve a purpose. Be clear what the purpose is and what needs to be decided or actioned at the meeting. Meetings should be chaired effectively and not last longer than necessary. It is doubtful whether people can concentrate for more than two hours continuously. If the agenda appears to require longer, think of timing such that there is a break in the middle, or think of forming several subgroups each to consider a subset of the agenda items.

Produce and keep a written record of all decisions taken and all actions agreed at meetings.

Internal progress reports should be brief and succinct, even in bullet point format, especially if they are to be tabled at a meeting where further information can be presented orally. Of course progress reports or interim reports prepared for Steering Group meetings will need to be longer in order to inform a wider range of stakeholders who may not themselves be closely involved with the project.

An important tool for monitoring the progress of the project is the project plan. In fact, the purpose of a project plan is not just to set out how the project will be scheduled but to provide a benchmark against which progress can be measured once the project is implemented. In particular, it should be consulted to check whether critical activities (see Chapter 6) have been started at the specified dates and whether milestones have been reached at the correct times. The project plan is an important working document. Everyone involved with the project should have a copy and the document should be tabled at every project review meeting. All reporting of progress (oral or written) should be referenced to the project plan.

Microsoft Project (described in Chapter 6) has the facility to produce what is known as 'tracking Gantt charts'. As the project progresses actual start and finish times for activities can be entered, which might be earlier or later than those scheduled. From this information, Microsoft Project produces a revised Gantt chart indicating how the timing of remaining activities, including the completion date, will be affected. Microsoft Project can also be employed to identify and test the impact of alternative scenarios, such as committing extra resources to an activity or making the existing resources work longer hours. However, such a sophisticated application of the software is probably not required for most social research projects.

Adopting the project plan and the accompanying responsibility chart as working documents does not merely assist in monitoring the project, but focuses attention on what needs to be done. It also minimises acrimony between team members. It is my experience that with a clear plan (which everyone has signed up to) team members are more proactive in scheduling their own work and more readily accept responsibility for any delays. Rather than blame others or find excuses, dialogue tends to be more constructive and focused on the way forward.

Maintaining quality of fieldwork, data collection and analysis

Quality was defined in Chapter 1 as fitness for purpose, indicating that quality is itself a relative concept. It is also multi-dimensional. The European Statistical System (as quoted in the *National Statistics Protocol of Quality Management* (http://www.statistics.gov.uk/about/national_statistics/cop/downloads/quality management.pdf)) identifies seven dimensions:

1   relevance
2   accuracy
3   timeliness
4   accessibility
5   comparability
6   coherence
7   completeness.

In response to general concerns about the quality of qualitative research, especially in regard to rigour and robustness, Government Social Researchers commissioned a framework for assessing qualitative research evidence (Spencer *et al.*, 2003). The framework was prepared primarily for the benefit of sponsors and users of research to enable them to make informed judgements of the findings of qualitative research. However, the framework is immensely useful to researchers and research managers in designing qualitative research studies and in implementing them. The authors identified five key quality issues and concerns surrounding qualitative research:

1   the defensibility of approach
2   the rigour of conduct
3   the relationship of the researcher to the research
4   the credibility of claims
5   the broader impact and contribution of the study.

The quality standard set for the research project will have been addressed in the initial proposal and in discussions with the funding or commissioning body. The design of the project and the methodology to be adopted will have been constructed to ensure that the quality standard is met. Thus obtaining quality is much about implementing and adhering to the prescribed methodology, for example, to ensure that:

- the target population is reached
- bias is not introduced in the selection of research subjects
- specified response rates are achieved
- questionnaires are clear and unambiguous
- bias is not introduced in the wording of questions
- in-depth interviews are conducted appropriately and professionally
- interviewees are not mislead during in-depth interviews
- focus groups are properly moderated
- ethnographic methods do not alter or influence the behaviour that is being observed and studied
- missing data is minimised
- qualitative and quantitative data are accurately collected and coded/ recorded
- qualitative and quantitative data are analysed fully, employing the appropriate analytical techniques
- all stages of the project are carried out objectively and researchers' personal beliefs have not unduly influenced the outcome.

Quality is also related to ethical conduct. Research subjects who are treated openly, honestly and sensitively are far more likely to participate and engage fully with the research. The nature and quality of their responses will be improved as a result of the respect and dignity being accorded to them.

Furthermore, it should be emphasised, that quality is to a large extent dependent on the skills and abilities of the project team, their professionalism and their commitment to the project. Thus all the points made in the first section of this chapter 'Managing the team', regarding training, motivating and creating a climate and culture that empowers team members and encourages openness and honesty, are also vitally important in achieving high quality.

The purpose here is not to discuss methodology: a vast number of texts exist on designing surveys and questionnaires, conducting in-depth interviews, running focus groups and on analysing qualitative and quantitative data. Ethical issues in social research are the subjects of Chapter 11 and managing the team was addressed above. The concern here is how to manage the data-gathering and analysis stage of the project to ensure that the methodology is carried out, ethical standards adhered to and quality obtained. (In so doing, it is recognised that it is not always possible to identify the division between methodology, ethics and management practice.)

Considerable attention is paid to defining the objectives of the project and in refining the methodology, which culminates in the signing of the contract. But it is my perception that insufficient attention is given to managing the fieldwork stage of a project, especially by sponsors or commissioners of research. I am not sure why this should be so, perhaps it is felt that once agreed, undertaking the data collection can simply be delegated, or perhaps because other tasks that have been neglected, now appear more pressing and are given attention. (It might simply stem from sheer fatigue of those involved in negotiating the contract.) Regardless of the cause, the potential for the project to go horribly wrong at this stage should not be ignored, as the following examples serve to illustrate.

Example 1   A study to evaluate a particular intervention involved interviewing participants before and after they took part in the programme. Unfortunately, the interviews were not date-stamped, so when it came to the analysis, before-interviews could not be distinguished from after-interviews.

Example 2   All victims of domestic violence who came to the notice of agencies over a period of time were interviewed. Domestic violence is a repeat offence so many victims reappeared during the study period. But they often gave different names (full names, nicknames) and addresses and it proved difficult to assemble the final dataset linking incidents and agency referrals to individuals.

Example 3   A study involved telephone interviews with the general public. Students and sessional workers were hired to conduct the interviews. They were given a quota of interviews to complete during the session and were paid a bonus for meeting that quota. The interview was to take 10–15 minutes but took nearer 30, leading many respondents to hang up part way through the interview. In these cases the interviewer went on to complete the questionnaire and in sessions where it was difficult to contact respondents, an entire questionnaire was fictitiously completed.

Example 4   At the point of undertaking statistical analysis confusion arose over the variables. One was thought, erroneously, to be measuring a specific phenomenon and was designated to be the dependent/response variable. Given the inter-correlation between many of the variables, plausible results emerged from the analysis. The problem was not spotted until the report was about to leave for the printers.

Example 5   An economic study was undertaken of rateable values of property across local authority areas. Having completed and reported the results one reader was suspicious of some of the values presented and persistently queried them. Eventually it was discovered that the decimal point had been put in the wrong place in many of the data fields and the values were incorrect.

I could give many other examples where interviewers have not fully understood the nature of their assignment and others where people have come to the wrong conclusions when undertaking secondary analysis through lack of an understanding of the dataset.

Do you think that these examples are exceptions and could not happen to you? They are all real projects that the researchers involved have related to me.

And the studies were undertaken by well-established and creditable research organisations, not untrained amateurs. Most of those relating these examples confessed that they had been humbled by the experience and it had certainly made them a good deal more wary and prepared in future.

Ensuring quality

Before commissioning research from an organisation or before embarking on a collaboration with another research organisation, assurances should be obtained that the organisation is able to deliver quality research and it is committed to doing so. Indicators commonly sought are whether the organisation has adopted and complies with a quality standard (in particular ISO 9000) or has qualified as Investors in People. If so, this will offer some guarantee that the organisation takes the issue seriously and has implemented systems to train staff, monitor and quality-assure work.

Financial viability and stability of the organisation is another criterion often applied. It is common for government departments to ask to see, and hence scrutinise, the last three annual accounts of the organisation.

Further important criteria to consider are the previous experience and reputation of the organisation, and, especially, the particular team who will be working on the project. Examples of previous research of a similar kind undertaken by the organisation/team can be most instructive in judging the quality standards attained. Do the team members belong to a professional body and do they adhere to the code of conduct of that body?

The criteria outlined above are among those discussed in Chapter 3 for evaluating proposals submitted in response to a competitive tender. Research managers should check whether his/her organisation has adopted certain quality standards and has available an infrastructure to support those standards.

The most highly regarded method of quality assurance in social research is peer review, and opportunities should be taken to expose one's research to the scrutiny of ones peers. If possible, and time permits, seek peer review before submitting the initial proposal (and sponsors may send proposals they have received for peer review – all applications to the ESRC are assessed in this way). All final reports are peer reviewed. End of Award Reports, based on the comments of academic assessors, are fed back to ESRC grant holders and most other sponsors seek external comments on reports they receive. And, of course, any paper submitted to a scientific journal will be refereed. At the implementation stage of the project, reaching peers through presentations of interim findings at workshops, seminars and conferences is a common course of action (although there may be contractual restrictions on how far results can be publicised before the research is completed). In addition, consider inviting one or two peers to join the Steering or Advisory Committee.

It is good practice to designate a person or persons as being responsible for quality assurance. The project manager will obviously take a lead but where possible a senior colleague, who is not a prominent member of the project team, should be appointed to independently assess that quality standards are being met. The remit to review quality should be clearly stated and time set aside to enable all concerned to adequately fulfil their roles. Time and effort should be costed and included in any proposal so that the person or the institution is adequately reimbursed for the work undertaken. The role should be viewed as an essential aspect of project management, not simply as a favour conferred by a friend as and if time permits.

As already mentioned, in social research project management it is the tendency not to formally adopt auditing, testing and reviewing procedures, although they are implicit in much that is done. However, I suggest that they should be planned and thought through a little more systematically than is current practice.

Quality reviews should be undertaken periodically. One option is to re-title several of the progress meetings 'Quality Review Meetings', where the purpose of the discussion is to assess the technical quality of the work. Making the separation between progress and quality, and not dealing with them both at one and the same time, often helps concentrate thinking and leads to a more productive meeting. Furthermore, an open but formal review of quality, in which all concerned can contribute, can appear less threatening to an individual team member whose component is being scrutinised than a one-to-one discussion with the line manager. Quality review meetings may well have a different membership and different submissions tabled than a routine progress meeting.

To maximise their impact, quality review meetings should be scheduled at key points in the project life cycle, often just prior to starting an activity, to ensure preparations have been completed (for example, the appropriate research instrument has been developed and agreed) and shortly after an activity has begun, to ensure that it is attaining the standard set, while there is still time to take any corrective action.

It is often beneficial for the colleague designated to help quality-assure the project to chair quality review meetings or at least be in attendance. Membership should extend to any stakeholder who would have a useful contribution to make to ensuring quality standards are met; such as gatekeepers to research subjects, representatives of the community being researched, experts in the data being collected and so on. Some stakeholders may already be members of the Steering Group. External composition of the quality review meetings will vary depending on the stage of the project and the focus of the review.

All research instruments should be tested (in social research parlance, piloted) prior to use but also again after they have been implemented – to gauge whether they are still working effectively, or that the changes made after piloting are acceptable. Protocols and procedures should also be audited.

What aspects of the fieldwork/data analysis ought to be quality-assured?

Data collection

- Ensure that all research instruments (questionnaires, discussion guides, coding frames) and other materials to be used in order to collect data are thoroughly prepared and have been scrutinised/tested/piloted.
- Ensure instructions for using the research instruments have been prepared, are clear and have been distributed and assimilated by those who are to collect the data.
- Ensure all interviewers/moderators/researchers have been properly briefed and trained.
- Audit procedures for selecting research participants.
- Monitor that interviewees are members of the target population and that participants in group discussions conform to the recruitment criteria – and that expected numbers have been interviewed/recruited.
- Ensure venues are suitable for interviews/qualitative group discussions – inspect the premises and ask interviewers/moderators for feedback on the venue and the arrangements for conducting the research.
- Validate interviews by re-contacting a sample of interviewees and asking whether the interview took place and what topics were covered. Telephone interviews can be validated by using remote listening equipment enabling the supervisor to 'be present' at the interview. Similarly re-contact a sample of participants in qualitative research to validate the nature and subject of the group discussion.
- Check procedures and any equipment to be used in recording discussions/ in-depth interviews.
- Visually inspect a sample of completed questionnaires, and a sample of field notes and records/recordings of any interviews/discussions.
- Observe data collection by listening in to telephone interviews (as already mentioned), accompanying interviewers, sitting in on focus group discussions or by extracting a sample of administrative data from files/databases.

In addition to these specific points, it is also necessary to consider 'fitness for purpose'. The data may be of high quality but is it the right data to address the issue and to answer the research question? Ensure that those who will be collecting the data fully understand the aims and objectives of the project and the wider context so that they are better able to judge what information is relevant. It may be helpful to include stakeholders in any discussions as they may bring specific knowledge or insight.

I should emphasise that the purpose of adopting the above procedures is not only to monitor the quality of the fieldwork, but to gain first-hand experience of the strengths and limitations of the methodology and of the data collected. This information will be invaluable when interpreting and contextualising the results of the subsequent analysis. There is no substitute for 'getting close to data collection' for the insights it can provide.

Finally, one should be particularly concerned about the procedures for ensuring the quality of data in studies addressing sensitive issues, such as illegal, deviant or stigmatised behaviour or studies that threaten the interests of research subjects or touch on embarrassing, confidential or personal matters.

Readers may wish to know that the Market Research Society has produced three guides that bear on quality, although their specific purpose is to set out how ethical principles translate into fieldwork practice. They are *MRS Code and Guidelines*:

Guidelines for Research Among Children and Young People
Quantitative Data Collection Research Guidelines
Qualitative Research Guidelines

All three are available at www.marketresearch.org.uk (click on code/guidelines). There is also the British Standard Organizations *Conducting Market Research (BS 7911 : 2003)* which sets out good practice procedures to be followed when conducting survey research.

Data processing and analysis

- Ensure each questionnaire, interview record, group discussion is appropriately labelled with unique identifiers and date stamped.
- Keep questionnaire, records/recordings for checking and in order to validate quotes, transcripts, content analysis or annotations (but be aware of any obligations under the Data Protection Act).
- Develop and apply range and logic checks to identify miscodings.
- Check that numbers of records processed equates with field returns – it is surprising how many questionnaires/records go missing. Check for duplicate identifiers – it is surprising how often data is entered twice.
- Check that data has in fact been recoded and labelled as intended and derived variables have been constructed correctly.
- Check record length (keying errors are often caused by a field not being entered throwing out the remainder of the record).
- Test for consistency/reliability between coders.
- Review how categories/themes have been derived from qualitative data.
- Review how qualitative data has been analysed. Is sufficient data presented to support findings? Should the analysis be repeated by more than one researcher to ensure reliability?
- Check that the base for any table is correct against other tables and that rows, columns and sub-totals sum correctly.
- Review whether the appropriate statistical techniques have been employed and that the data have been analysed thoroughly.

In addition to the checklist given above, I make a point when analysing data collected by others to contact those who did collect it in order to enquire about any issues that might be pertinent to any analysis that I might be proposing. When collecting data from administrative records I try to make myself as familiar as possible with the definitions of the data items, how the data was collected, by whom and for what purpose. This is especially important if any comparative analysis is to be undertaken, as different organisations will adopt slightly different definitions, rules and recording procedures for the same item of information. Even information that appears unambiguous can turn out on close inspection to be problematic. To take but one example, death from road accidents – which most people would consider as leaving little scope for ambiguity. However, in this country, cause of death is recorded as a road accident if death occurs within thirty days of the accident (and this is becoming the international standard). But in Italy the death has to be within seven days and Japan one day for the cause to be recorded as a road accident. In Switzerland it can be as much as one year after the accident.

Despite best endeavours it is still possible to be 'caught out'. As part of a study I was given data by a police force on the number of crime scenes visited by forensic scientists. Analysed alongside other data, this data was presented in the final report of the project. The force queried the figures, which did not conform to their own records. Fearing the worst and that my reputation was at stake, I spent many days checking data entry and what subsequent operations I had performed on the data. Eventually it transpired that the force had two counts, one where forensic scientists left the station and physically visited the location of the crime and one where forensic scientists examined items from a crime scene, including those items that may have been brought into the laboratory from the scene. (In terms of my interest, a measure of how many crime scenes receive an examination from a forensic scientist, a case can be made for either count.)

Reliability can often be more of a problem than error, and this is often brought about by different researchers coding data in slightly different ways. Unwanted variability is introduced. Minimising this variability can be achieved by developing comprehensive coding instructions and any items not covered by the instructions should be referred to a central point where they can be reviewed and a consistent decision taken. All decisions should be formally recorded.

Last, but by no means least, think about the security of the data, at all stages of the project. This important issue should be considered as part of any risk analysis and was also touched upon in Chapter 9 when safety was discussed and in Chapter 10 under confidentiality and data protection. Nevertheless, while an obvious point, losing data will adversely affect the quality of the project.

The important topic of quality assuring the outputs of the project, in particular written reports, is discussed in the next chapter.

9 Dissemination

Throughout their careers researchers will be called upon to write proposals and reports and to make oral presentations to sponsors, policy makers, practitioners, peers, the media and the public at large. Effective dissemination can thus win a contract in the first place, keep customers and stakeholders informed and happy throughout the project and ultimately advance knowledge, influence policy and practice as well as enhancing the reputation of the team and the research institute.

Dissemination should be regarded and managed in the same way as any other aspect of the project:

- a dissemination strategy should be formulated
- plans drawn up to implement the strategy
- resources allocated
- progress monitored against the plan.

Having emphasised the need to plan and manage dissemination, I fully appreciate that it is not uncommon for plans to be revised in the light of the results of the research or as a result of increased interest shown in the subject matter of the research. Researchers can find themselves and their research thrust into the centre of a controversy which is attracting the attention of the media. This can present a welcome opportunity to inform a current debate in a neutral and dispassionate manner although, equally, the researchers can find themselves in an uncomfortable crossfire and being labelled as a supporter or protagonist of a particular party promoting its own self interests. (I write from experience having written a report in the late 1980s on the effects of imprisonment in reducing crime only to find an updated version of it reported on the front page of the *Guardian* (15 October 1993) in an attempt to discredit the then Home Secretary's latest policy initiative.)

Dissemination strategy

The objective of dissemination is to maximise the impact of the project by getting the messages across to those who could benefit from the research or to those who simply need to be informed.

It is important to be clear at the outset what the funder or sponsor expects, permits or prohibits in terms of dissemination by the researchers themselves. Funders have very different views. The ESRC positively encourages the researchers to disseminate findings from their studies, so much so that plans for dissemination have to be included in the initial application and dissemination is one criterion on which an application is judged (see Chapter 4). Government departments, at the other extreme, prefer to handle dissemination of the research they sponsor themselves. Charities fall somewhere in between. As a general rule, private companies tend to wish to control outputs from research they sponsor, although it is for the company itself to decide and there are exceptions to the rule.

The ESRC offers advice and support to its grant holders and it has also produced and published *Four Guides to Disseminating Results*:

1   *Developing a Media Strategy*
2   *Television and Radio: A best practice guide*
3   *Influencing the Policy Process*
4   *Heroes of Dissemination*.

All four are available at the ESRC website by entering the titles in the search box.

In addition, the ESRC has produced an excellent Communications Toolkit, which is available at www.esrc.ac.uk/commstoolkit/intro.asp (a link is also available at the ESRC home page) and includes a template to be used in formulating a communications strategy. The Toolkit also contains tips on how to engage the media and deal with queries, how to brand and market research, prepare events and how to develop websites. These specialist topics are not considered further here except to point out that most institutions have a press officer who will help to develop and implement the strategy to engage the media, prepare documentation and help deal with queries. The press officer should thus be consulted. Similarly, most institutions will have a website and a designated person responsible for its development and maintenance. The issue will thus be to negotiate with that person how best to incorporate information on the project into the existing website.

What follows sets out the issues that need to be thought through in formulating a dissemination strategy.

First, identify all stakeholders and other potential target audiences that need to be reached. The objective of the stakeholder analysis is to ascertain who needs to know, who should know and who might be interested to know of the existence of the project, its progress and outcome. The analysis should clarify with regard to each group:

•   what particular aspects of the project they are interested in or ought to know about

- when they would want to receive the information or when it is most appropriate to deliver it
- in what form they would prefer to receive the information
- how they are to be approached and contacted about the project.

Dissemination has to be tailored to meet the requirements of a specific stakeholder/audience. The sponsor and members of the project Steering Committee will need regular written and perhaps oral updates on progress, briefing on emerging findings and a final written report. At the other extreme, disseminating results to practitioners or the informed public may best be achieved by a short article in an appropriate newsletter or 'trade magazine' concentrating on those aspects of most relevance to that particular group. Providing feedback to the subjects of the research needs to be considered, individual participants will appreciate a short leaflet summarising the results of the research whereas participating organisations or professional associations may well wish to receive the full report. (They may receive it through their membership of the Steering or Advisory Group.)

Alternatively (or in addition) the audience can be reached by an oral presentation at a suitable gathering. In my time I have given talks amongst others to magistrates, probation and police officers, forensic scientists and the Parole Board at their annual conferences, regional meetings or training courses. There are always opportunities to reach users through their own channels and forums. The internet provides an important medium for dissemination and more and more information is being published 'online'. Creating a web page about the research is an easy and cost effective method of reaching a worldwide audience. Reaching the wider public invariably involves working with and through the media and preparing Press Releases. Communicating with peers is also via written articles in academic journals.

Having drawn up details of who needs to know what and when and the means by which the information is to be disseminated, the next step is to formulate a dissemination plan. This plan is no different in conception to project plans discussed in Chapter 6 and should have similar characteristics, that is, lists of specific activities or actions that need to be taken, durations (time to complete the task), completion dates and persons identified as being responsible for undertaking the task.

In order to implement the plan, a list of contact names and addresses will need to be assembled. Many contacts will be obvious and their details known, for example groups funding or participating in the project and those represented on the Steering Committee. But others will not be immediately apparent, such as other groups not directly involved, or journalists and other media contacts.

Procedures for monitoring progress will need to be established. Dissemination can be a standing item on the internal team meetings or Steering Committee meetings. This will ensure that progress is reviewed routinely along with other aspects of the project. (Even if for many early meetings there is nothing to report and the item is not taken, at least dissemination will not be overlooked.) It is quite possible, of course, that much of the dissemination will occur after the project has ended and the Steering Committee (perhaps even the research team) has disbanded. The salience of a project or its full impact may not be apparent until some time after the project has concluded, perhaps when other, related, research has been completed or the government or other public body initiates a public consultation on the subject area. The plan may well need to extend beyond the life of the project and thought will need to be given about how the strategy can be continued into the future.

To implement the plan, resources will be required, in the form of time and effort of the research team but also time and effort of others (such as designers and writers of publicity material and the institution's press and information officers). This effort will cost money. The ESRC recommends in its Communications Toolkit that around 5 per cent of the total funded research budget should be allocated for dissemination and communication.

Report writing

One output from a social research project, and one medium through which findings are disseminated, is a written report. There are many forms of a report but in the context of social research, I take a report to be an objective and professional account of the design of the study and its findings, the conclusions that can be drawn and the implications and recommendations that may stem from them.

There are three aspects to producing a report:

* determining the kind of report to be written
* managing the process of writing the report
* layout and style of the report.

Determining the kind of report to be written

The first question to ask is who is the intended audience for the report? What are their levels of understanding, what do they need to know, what messages do you want to get across to them? These questions will have been addressed when formulating the dissemination strategy and are not considered further here, apart to say that one report will probably not meet the needs of every intended audience. It is more than probable that several reports will need to be produced.

A 'full' or 'final' report documenting all aspects of the project should be written and this is a requirement of funding bodies. The ESRC requires an End of Award Report to be submitted and researchers may eventually publish a revised version of it as a book. Sponsoring charities and government departments will require a final report, which they then publish in their own research series.

Full does not mean long. The length should be no longer than needed to adequately document the research. Sponsors are increasingly stipulating the maximum length of the report to be submitted to them. And they are also requesting the report contains an Executive Summary.

Most government departments now follow the practice initiated by the Joseph Rowntree Foundation of publishing separately the Research Findings, a four-page (2,500 word) summary of the report. These summaries are intended to reach a wider audience who are interested in the subject matter, the main findings and any implications, but not the detail of the research.

In our rush to influence the busy policy maker or reach the ubiquitous person on the Clapham omnibus, we should not neglect the need to report the research in a scientifically rigorous way in order that it can be professionally assessed and take its place in the body of knowledge. It is well to remember that most systematic reviews or meta analyses of previous research end up discarding a lot of potential informative studies because the reports of them contain insufficient detail of the design of the study and of the data generated. Reaching an academic audience is still best achieved through referred journal articles where the emphasis is on the scientific rigour and the ultimate long-term value of the research.

Any or all of these reports may or may not be published in paper form and/or electronically on the web.

Managing the process of writing the report(s)

First be clear what kinds of reports are to be prepared and when. This should have been determined when formulating the dissemination strategy or when negotiating the final contract with the sponsor (see Chapter 5). As part of those negotiations clarify with sponsors their rules regarding length and house style. Some government departments have produced guides for authors and a good example is *Writing for RDS: A guide for authors*, prepared by the Home Office Research and Statistics Directorate and freely available at their website (www.homeoffice.gov.uk/rds/guide_to_authors.html). The Joseph Rowntree Foundation has also produced *Publication and Dissemination: A guide for JRF projects*, available at (www.jrf.org.uk/funding/research/projectholders/documents/panddguide.doc). Read any guidance produced by the sponsor early in the project life cycle and clarify any misunderstandings you may have.

Plan to begin writing the report at the earliest opportunity and write additional sections of the report as the project progresses. Do not leave all the report writing to the last minute. In Chapter 2, receiving a badly written report was highlighted by commissioners of research as a major problem, the inference being drawn that researchers could not write. My interpretation is slightly different. Problems arise because insufficient time has been allowed for the preparation of the report. The problem is usually exacerbated by delays in starting the project so that towards the end there is a rush to complete the analysis as well as write the report (and often one of the research team has left to take up another position so as not to be out of work when his/her contract expires). The upshot is that in order to meet the deadline, the researchers submit the hastily produced first draft of the report when they should be submitting a more polished third draft. A first draft will never be good enough so allow time to produce subsequent drafts. Was it Churchill who said words to the effect that 'had I had more time I would have written less', emphasising the point that it takes a lot longer to produce a succinct and well-written report?

Hastily prepared inadequate reports can easily be avoided. Sections of the report can be written well in advance of the project completion date. Once the project has been agreed the aims and objectives can be written, together with any background context for the research (although this may need updating as events occur or other research is published). Sections on research design/ methodology and fieldwork/data collection can be written as soon as they have been formulated and completed. In fact, only the sections relating to the final analysis, conclusions, implications and recommendations cannot be written prior to the last few weeks of any project. The earlier one starts preparing the final report the better. A research manager I work with immediately draws up an outline of the final report once his proposal has been accepted. He then 'cuts and pastes' relevant sections of his proposal into appropriate places in, what will become, the final report.

Draw up a plan to identify when each section of the report(s) needs to be written, who will write that section, who will comment on it (and perhaps redraft it) and who will quality-assure it. The report plan can then be integrated with the project plan and linked in with project activities and milestones. An effective procedure is to write sections of any final report alongside preparing a progress report or an interim report. Sections of the final report can then be submitted with the other required report and feedback obtained. Time will then be available to redraft the report in the light of comments received.

By scheduling sufficient time it will be possible to allocate responsibility for writing sections of the report to junior or inexperienced staff. It is important to give such staff every opportunity to develop their report writing skills but also to identify and take ownership of the work. However, it is likely that their draft will need extensive rewriting, which can only be achieved if time permits.

Consider how the report will be quality-assured. The best method is to engage someone who is familiar with social research and has experience of writing research reports, but who is independent of the project, to read the report. A suitable person might be a senior colleague in the organisation/ institution. They must have sufficient authority and confidence to be objective and critical. It serves no one's interests to engage someone who is inhibited from saying what they genuinely believe. It is sometimes possible for one of the research team to fulfil this role, but only if they have not been involved in the project day-to-day nor written large sections of the report. Detachment is essential.

To undertake the task properly, time must be made available. Quality assurance is not just a quick read through. Formal checks need to be made to ensure the report is internally consistent. Common problems include:

- different titles and spellings to describe previous research studies, public documents and institutions
- tables and diagrams not consistently labelled and referenced
- data in tables not adding up
- totals varying between tables when they should not.

If possible, a person to quality-assure the report should have been identified at the proposal stage and costs included to cover that commitment. The person (or his or her institution) should be reimbursed for the time they spend on quality assurance. As discussed in Chapter 8, quality assurance should be an integral part of any project and not seen as a favour to be sought from a friend or trusted colleague at the end of the project.

Structure and style

The structure and style will depend, to a degree, on the type of report and the audience it is intended to reach. Spend time planning a clear and appropriate structure for the report.

When writing a short summary or Research Findings style of report, intended for 'busy people', start with the main messages stemming from the study. (This convention is mandatory for press releases, or ministerial submissions.) The messages can be set out in bullet format. The reader's attention must be grabbed at the outset and he or she encouraged to read further. (If they cannot or will not read any further at least they have received the main messages.)

The next section should give the context to the research and emphasise why the research being reported is salient to current debates and issues. Later sections should expand on the findings of the research and describe the methodology to the research.

The structure of a full report will be different, although it is still important to get over the main messages clearly and early in the report. The practice of including an Abstract at the beginning of a journal article and an Executive Summary in a full report are intended to meet that objective.

A logical order for the full report is often self-evident; consisting of an explanation of the issue being examined (and set in its wider context), how the research was carried out, the data collected and analysed, conclusions, implications and recommendations (if any). It is perhaps more important, therefore, to consider navigational aids, linking passages, summaries and consistency. Remember many readers do not read each page in sequence starting at page 1, but use the contents page or the Executive Summary to dictate how they will read subsequent sections and in what order. If the report has been prepared by more than one member of the team, or has had a long gestation period (as recommended above), inconsistencies will be inevitable. The person who is to quality-assure the report should be instructed to consider all these matters.

Structure may vary according to the type of report, but there are some universal stylistic points which should be observed. These can be summarised as:

- language should be clear and concise (use short, familiar words, avoid jargon, clichés, fashionable or vogue words and unnecessary words)
- use the active tense, which makes the prose move faster
- using the first person (I and we) is acceptable (despite what many of us were taught at school)
- avoid long paragraphs
- keep sentences short (one idea or meaning per sentence).

The Home Office guide *Writing for RDS: A guide for authors*, referred to above, contains much useful information on style, including detailed guidance on punctuation and spelling (and common misspellings). And, of course, the classic in the use of English remains Gowers (1948).

Chapman and Wykes (1996) provide valuable guidance on presenting numeric data – a neglected topic in most guides, which concentrate on the written word. In most social research projects many tables and charts will have been produced at the analysis stage by a computer package, notably SPSS or Excel. A temptation, and unfortunately an increasingly common practice, is to cut and paste these into the report. Resist the temptation – the tables produced are not suitable, at least not in their raw form.

Chapman and Wykes' advice is to decide what they call the verbal summary first, that is, the text that will accompany the table or chart (and there should always be a written commentary accompanying a table/chart). The text will help to decide the form of table or chart. Do not try to convey too much information in a table/chart or make it too dense (they can always be broken down into further tables and charts). Embed tables/charts in the main body of the text rather than relegate them to an annex.

- Tables/charts should be clearly numbered and precisely headed stating which variables are tabulated.
- The source of the data and the date of when the data were collected should be stated in the heading or at the foot of the table.
- Give the total or sample size and any weighted sample size (if the data have been weighted).
- Give the number of cases or people excluded from the table and who these are.
- Tables should contain few lines, usually no more than four horizontal lines to separate the heading from the table, the column headings from the data and one at the bottom of the table. (Another might be used to distinguish the total from the rows.) Vertical lines should generally be avoided.
- Align the numbers appropriately.

- Label axes fully, with units of measurement if appropriate.
- The eye prefers to compare vertically rather than horizontally, and round numbers in order to facilitate comparison.
- Arrange columns and rows, where possible in some natural order (e.g. years chronologically) or, if there is no natural order (e.g. membership of a religious group) arrange in descending order of size of membership.

Whether to use charts, and which kind of chart is a matter of preference, the main issue to be addressed is whether it succeeds in clearly conveying the meaning and in making the intended point. Colour provides many more options and contrasting colours can make a visual impact. Colour is not always available, however, and documents are often photocopied in black and white negating the impact from the contrasting colours.

Personally I prefer bar charts to pie charts. Like most people, I prefer horizontal bar charts to vertical ones – unless data for different years are being compared. Just as with rows and columns in tables, arrange bars in a natural order or descending size order. I like line charts to convey trends.

Oral presentations

Oral presentations should be regarded very differently from written reports. The spoken word is not the same as the written word and people are accustomed to receive information differently through the ear than through the eye. As a consequence it is not possible to convey so much information in an oral presentation as in a written report. Oral messages should be shorter, simpler and less complex. People's attention span is limited and, unlike a written report, there is no opportunity to re-read certain passages, put it down, take a break and return to it when the reader wishes, or even to read sections in the order preferred by the reader as opposed to the order of the writer's choosing. It is also more difficult to convey detailed information orally than in writing. Finally, an oral presentation has the added ingredient of the individual (or individuals) making the presentation; their appearance, manner and voice are all part of the event.

The main inferences to be drawn from these, perhaps obvious, points are that a presentation should be prepared to be heard not read. An oral presentation should be limited to getting over the main messages and a small number of essential points. Detailed information can be put in handouts, or made available on the web or by reference to the written report should one exist. Thought needs to be given to the performance of the presenter(s).

Planning a presentation

Planning a particular presentation, the Principal Researcher or Team Leader should be clear about:

- the purpose of the presentation
- the size and composition of the likely or intended audience
- the location/venue, its layout, facilities and equipment
- the length of the presentation.

Taking each bullet in turn, who initiated the presentation and what purpose did they have in mind? You may have initiated it, if so why?

Who is attending the presentation? Will the audience be small, such as members of the commissioning panel for the research, or the project Steering Committee – who will be knowledgeable, have a keen interest in the work and are likely to ask a number of detailed and challenging questions? Or, at the other extreme, is the presentation to a large audience who will come to the presentation with little background knowledge and only a tangential interest in the detail of the research? In small gatherings it is appropriate to invite questions while you are presenting, but this is not a good idea with a large audience.

Where is the presentation to take place? Around a table in a small meeting room or in a large auditorium or lecture theatre arranged 'conference style' with rows of seats facing in the same direction? What facilities are available or are needed, protectors, amplification systems or hearing loops?

The time allocated for the presentation is invariably determined and known in advance if it forms part of a larger conference or seminar programme. However, if the allotted time is not clearly specified (such as when presenting to a Steering Group meeting), settle and agree this in advance with the organisers, Chair or Secretary or another appropriate person.

Clarifying these initial four points will help focus upon and answer the following:

- What outcomes does the presentation need to achieve?
- Which member(s) of the team should attend the presentation?
- Which member(s) of the team should present and on what aspects?

What outcomes does the presentation need to achieve?

It is important to be clear what outcomes are expected or desired. Others may have requested the presentation for a specific purpose and the presentation may form part of a general meeting to discuss or resolve issues. Nevertheless, always consider what other objectives you may wish to achieve. These might include: to win the contract, to gain cooperation and agreement to certain actions, to facilitate access to data/research subjects, to resolve problems, to obtain additional time or resources, to persuade or influence, to report progress, raise awareness or to impart knowledge. Of course they are not mutually exclusive and a presentation could achieve more than one outcome.

Which member(s) of the team should attend the presentation?

As a general rule I believe the Principal Researcher/Team Leader or at the very least his or her deputy should attend and make a significant contribution to the presentation, but that every opportunity should be seized to involve other team members, especially junior members of the team as and when appropriate. It is never acceptable, in my view, to send junior team members to present on their own and without support to the Steering Committee or similar groups, which can be challenging and unnerving especially if the researcher is out-numbered (as is usually the case) or confronted by those occupying senior positions.

Depending on the size of the team or the purpose of the meeting, especially if it would incur a large time commitment and travel costs, not every one need attend but a large turnout should be considered for any presentation that has been arranged as part of the initial tendering process. Sponsors like to see and meet the team that will be actively working on the project.

On other occasions it is important for some staff to attend to receive acknowl-edgement for their work, to hear the discussion or to simply gain experience of such events. I would always look to take junior staff to meetings with ministers or senior officials if research, and particularly their research, was to be presented and discussed.

Which member(s) of the team should present and on what aspects?

As above, the Principal Investigator should expect to play a prominent part in any presentation, although that does not mean that he or she has to speak for the longest period of time. His or her role may be more to conduct proceedings, to make sure it runs to plan and to help all team members if required. The Principal Investigator should certainly be on hand to deal with any 'tricky' questions or difficult situations. And only the Principal Investigator can take or agree to certain decisions that affect the project.

Presentations that try to give every team member a part often do not come over well. They are too disjointed with too many irritating breaks as speakers change positions at the lectern. On the other hand, having more than one presenter, especially for a long presentation, can work well as the change has the effect of re-engaging the audience, especially if the second speaker has a contrasting voice or presentation style.

Junior staff should be encouraged to present on their component of the research, even if they have little experience of presenting and are apprehensive about the role. Like all performing, presenting becomes easier through practice and from gaining experience. Joining a panel after the presentation to answer questions and deal with queries is one way of involving junior staff and of giving them more experience.

Preparation

Preparation is key to effective presentation, not all risks can be eliminated but they can be minimised. Be aware that preparation takes time, time to review, reflect and amend.

First, decide and write down what points or facts are essential and must be covered in the presentation. Do not pack too much into a presentation. Next, arrange the points into a logical sequence starting with an effective opening that will grab the audience's attention. Start by saying what you want to say and conclude by telling the audience what it is that you have told them. Consider summarising and recapping at key points within the presentation and at the end and finish with a powerful conclusion.

Think of the audience not yourself, then reflect on the level of knowledge of the audience and how much detail they require and how much knowledge they can be presumed to have. This will help pitch the presentation at the appropriate level. Consider how the points and arguments are to be conveyed. People like examples, metaphors and analogies. Are visual aids, graphics or supplementary handouts required? If you intend to show web pages at the presentation download these onto disk beforehand. Do not rely on calling them up during the presentation.

Having prepared the presentation, rehearse giving it – and, rehearse it more than once. Try to make one rehearsal at least as near to a full dress rehearsal as possible, with other team members or others in your organisation forming the audience. If possible audio record or video the rehearsal, play it back, note where improvements need to be made and make them. Above all use the rehearsal to check the length of the presentation and that all overheads and visual aids are correct (order and spelling, etc.) and can be seen and read at the back of the room and in the lighting conditions that will prevail at the venue.

In order to ensure that the presentation will go well some knowledge of the venue is vital. A full dress rehearsal at the venue is ideal, but this is not always possible. Often, you may already know the venue having presented (or attended presentations) there before. If the venue is not familiar to you or you cannot make a pre-visit at least get someone to describe it to you over the phone; its size, layout and facilities/equipment, etc. Whatever one's state of knowledge, get to the venue early so that equipment can be set up and tested. I cannot count the number of times I have turned up to a presentation only for the audience to be told to be patient and wait 15 minutes while a technician is found to sort out why the presenter's disk will not work on the venues' equipment. I thought that these 'glitches' were a thing of the past now that everyone had become more accustomed to operating such equipment. Not so. During the time I was writing this book I attended two training courses (on unrelated topics). At the first, the speaker's electronic presentation did not project properly onto the screen. Each slide had a light coloured background, the text was contained within boxes of a darker shade than the background. The boxes were blank, the text in them could not be seen. Yet, the presenter kept apologetically saying, the presentation had worked perfectly on the previous occasion at another venue in another town on different equipment. The problem at the second was not the electronic presentation but the photocopying of the slides, which were handed to the attendees. Information at the top, bottom and sides had been omitted.

Moral? Check every detail and leave nothing to chance, even if it has worked satisfactorily in the past. Prepare your fallback position: assuming that the equipment does not work, what will you do?

Finally, you will need to plan what you will wear and how you will appear. Consider how your appearance will be perceived by the audience. Is that how you want to be perceived? As a general rule you will not go wrong if you are a slight 'cut above' what everyone else is wearing. Dressing-up is safer than dressing-down. I once recall an applicant attending an interview for a post at the Home Office wearing a t-shirt and jeans. Neither I nor the other members of the panel objected to such attire (it's not uncommon for people to come to work similarly dressed on occasion) but it did affect our perception of the candidate. We did reflect on his judgement and what it might have indicated about his attitude towards the job.

Delivery

Presentation is a performing art and like all performances improvement comes with training, practice and experience. Everyone is nervous early in their careers, but take opportunities to speak, as only from experience will nerves subside. Not that all nervous tension is bad. The great cricketer, Jack Hobbs, said that if he wasn't a bit nervous when he went out to bat he would be out first ball. Some nerves are required to get the adrenalin flowing. What one wants to avoid is becoming paralysed as a result of being too nervous. The latter will only be achieved through experience.

Merely reading a prepared script tends not to make for a good presentation, better to use notes. Many good speakers will order the notes on hand-held cards (post-card size), but, if using such cards make sure the print is easily read, the cards are numbered and secured in order with a treasury tag. (If you drop them they will at least remain in the correct order.) It is common now to display those notes as powerpoint slides. Do not attempt to put too much on a slide and avoid the temptation of putting all the information on the screen and simply reading from it. This can become little better than reading from a prepared script. Also avoid using too many overheads or slides. Find times within the presentation to speak to the audience without the visual supports. It can be effective (and appreciated) to address the audience at the beginning for a few minutes before launching into using visual supports.

Memorise your opening few sentences or your opening two minutes. This will get you over those initial nerves that come from hearing your own voice and realising 'this is it, there's no going back'. The nerves tend to die down once you are 'up and running' if you get off to a good start.

Do not be afraid to show emotion, audiences respond to real people. Reveal passion, enthusiasm and commitment for subject matter and joy and pleasure in being there. The audience will not be attentive or respond (at least positively) if you do not show any interest in the topic or imply that giving the presentation is a chore you would have avoided if possible. Try and moderate your voice, by including some high and lows and pauses can be effective, as can taking a drink of water while the audience is left to fully reflect upon the importance of your last point. (Taking a drink of water is also a useful method of recovering the moment if you freeze.)

Hand movements and gestures, like removing glasses (or putting them on to read a quote), can be an effective way to emphasise a point. But avoid over dramatics and endlessly fiddling with something, such as a pen. The first is likely to make you come across as insincere and the second will make you seem nervous (which you probably are) and distracting for the audience. Train yourself not to say um and ah – just pause instead. Casting some parts of the presentation in a lighter vein and not always being too serious is a good strategy, but take care with jokes, make sure that they will be received in the way intended – and that they are funny. Certainly do not try too many.

Make sure that your voice carries to all parts of the room or auditorium and that you can be heard clearly (and that your visual aids can be seen – but this should have been resolved when preparing the presentation).

Stay within the time limit set. If you look to be hopelessly over (which you should not be if you prepared thoroughly) look to cut sections or shorten sections, do not simply talk faster to speed up the presentation.

Close by summarising the main points or the questions/issues that you want the audience to take away from the presentation. Think of an impressive memorable closing statement.

Learn from experience and learn from other speakers. All presentations are different and all offer lessons for the future. Try and get feedback from the organisers, co-presenters or from members of the audience. Was a colleague or associate in the audience who can comment? Even the best presenters 'bomb' on occasion. If it happens, learn the lessons and move on.

10 Intellectual property, copyright, confidentiality and data protection

> Intellectual property is an example of intangible personal property. It is a collection of ideas and information in a broadly commercial context that the law recognises as having a value by providing protection.
>
> (Hart and Fazzani, 2000)

The government's intellectual property website (www.intellectual-property. gov.uk) states 'intellectual property allows people to own their creativity and innovation in the same way that they can own physical property' and goes on to point out that there are four main types of IP:

- patents for inventions
- trade marks for brand identity
- designs for product appearance
- copyright for material – literary and artistic material, music, films, sound recordings and broadcasts, including software and multimedia, and database rights.

There are other types of IP (for example, trade secrets and performers' rights) but the main type that applies to social research is copyright and is the only type of IP considered in depth here.

Before discussing copyright it is worth noting an issue which can arise at the stage of commissioning research when several researchers or research groups have been asked to submit a tender to undertake a specific piece of research. The situation can arise, and often does, where a 'good idea' for conducting the research is proposed by one group but the commissioning body favours another group to undertake the work because on the balance of all the criteria set out to judge proposals the latter group's idea is considered to be the better. There is a temptation in the post-tender negotiations to suggest that the winning team amend their proposal to include the good idea contained in one of the other, losing, bids. (This issue was also discussed in Chapter 3.) The question often asked is whether such a suggestion infringes the intellectual property rights of the group who proposed the good idea. The short answer from a legal perspective is often no, but one should still consider the ethics of passing on one researcher's ideas to another, and issues of confidentiality.

The precise answer in any given circumstance will depend on the nature of the good idea. In most cases it falls into one of two categories; the researcher is either proposing an adaptation and application of a well-known methodology and approach to the research question or they are proposing to use a specific research instrument or database that they have developed. In the first they have not developed or created a distinctly new methodology so their intellectual property has not been infringed. In the second they will own rights in their research instrument or database (see below) and would be required to grant permission for others to use it or gain access to it – it could not simply be handed to another group.

Government researchers commissioning research on behalf of their department face this dilemma and in reaching a decision apply the test of whether other professional researchers could be expected to come up with the same good idea. If the answer is yes then it indicates that the good idea is not unique to the group proposing it and is thus not their intellectual property. However, there are important ethical considerations. How proper is it to pass on good ideas offered in confidence by one group to another? Again the answer depends on the nature of the good idea. If it was so good and unique (even if not constituting IP) why was the group not chosen for the work? If the answer to that question is that the group did not appear to have the project management or fieldwork skills to complete the work to a sufficiently high standard or were felt to incur greater risk of failure, one solution might be to suggest that the two groups work jointly on the project. Another ethical consideration (which some would say is also a contractual issue) is that by changing the nature of the research from that originally set out in the specification of requirement, or by making significant changes to a proposal from one research supplier, invalidates the original competition. If such changes are contemplated, some would argue that the requirement should be redefined and the competition rerun. Certainly there have been situations where one has felt that the competition was to identify the contractor and the work was specified afterwards in negotiations with that contractor.

Copyright

The position on copyright can cause a lot of confusion. It is important to bear in mind that data relevant to social science research will usually automatically be protected by copyright as well as the reports written during the course of the research.

There are various kinds of works which can be protected by copyright, although in the case of research conducted by social scientists, the most likely works to be relevant are literary works, datasets (and perhaps software) and sound and video recordings. The key issue of ownership relates to the creation of an original work, over which copyright is automatically created (unlike some other forms of IP where IP rights have to be applied for, registered and granted).

To be original, a work will usually be sufficiently different so as not to constitute a copy of something else. However, a work may still be original even if it is exactly the same as another work provided it can be demonstrated that is was created independently and not by copying. A work is original if it 'originated' with the author and if the author expended sufficient skill, labour and judgement in its creation. Thus, two people can take photographs of the same view, in the same lighting, such that the end results are identical, and each owns a copyright in their respective photographs. Except for limited circumstances, copyright lasts for 70 years after the end of the year in which the author dies. Therefore, copyright can apply to historical as well as contemporary data.

In England and Wales, copyright is governed by the 1988 Copyright, Designs and Patents Act and as amended, including, by the Copyright and Rights in Databases Regulations 1997 and the European Union Copyright Directive which was implemented into UK law in 2003.

Owners of copyright in a work have the right to prevent the following *unauthorised* acts:

- copying or otherwise exploiting the work
- issuing copies of the work to the public
- broadcasting the work or showing the work in public
- making an adaptation of the work.

These acts, if not authorised by the copyright owner, are known as 'infringement of copyright'. It is important to understand that copyright owners are free to authorise uses of data which would otherwise constitute infringement. Such authorisation is often referred to as a 'licence'.

In addition to copyright protection, authors may also have certain *moral rights* including the right to require that they are identified as author of a work, and the right to ensure that work is not treated in a derogatory way. (An example of derogatory treatment might be a serious study of sexual behaviour presented in the popular press in a trivial and sensationalised way.) However, the right to be identified as author must be asserted in writing, such as is often seen at the front of a book.

Crown Copyright

Material created by an officer or servant of the Crown in the course of his/ her duties is protected by 'Crown copyright'. Her Majesty the Queen is the owner of Crown copyright. Unlike normal copyright, Crown copyright lasts for 125 years from the date on which the work is created or 50 years from first commercial publication (subject to a maximum of 125 years' protection). This right includes documents created by civil servants.

Since March 1999, while continuing to assert its copyright to prevent misuse, the Crown has waived Crown copyright in certain categories of material, subject to limited exceptions. The material includes all primary and secondary legislation; government press notices, forms, consultative documents and high level statistics; published scientific, technical and medical papers; and unpublished public records.

The waiver of copyright in public records applies to information which is Crown copyright and which is contained in public records that were unpublished prior to deposit and that are available to the public. The information may be transcribed, translated, indexed and published, and photocopies may be reproduced, for any purpose, without the need for permission or acknowledgement. The waiver does not apply to published Crown copyright material; to material not in Crown copyright; to non-public records; or to photographic or digital images of documents created by the relevant repository. Advice on the application of the waiver and the exceptions is available from HMSO or the Public Record Office.

Ownership

Copyright in a work is first owned by the author of that work, subject to the employee/employer rules set out below. Copyright owners are free to assign the copyright to others, but assignments must be in writing. Copyright can also pass on death.

Researchers need to determine who owns copyright of the material on which they are working. It is illegal to use material without authorisation of the copyright owner. Whilst it is always better to obtain written authorisation, in many cases authorisation can be implied by the circumstances surrounding collection or creation of the material. Sometimes, but not always, it is obvious who owns the copyright. The law can differ as it relates to quantitative and qualitative data. Some key points to note are set out in the following paragraphs.

The design of a new questionnaire will almost certainly be protected by copyright. Copyright rests with the creator of that questionnaire. Multiple-choice answers provided by interviewees to pre-coded questions are not considered original works and copyright in this type of raw data rests with the interviewer.

Interviewees own copyright in answers to open-ended questions. If those answers are summarised by the interviewer in such a way as to create a new original work, then copyright in that new work (the summary) rests with the interviewer. However, if those answers are written down as substantially the same words as those spoken by the interviewee or reproduced verbatim then no new work is created and copyright in the written answer belongs to the interviewee. However, use of material by the interviewer may be covered by fair dealing clauses (see below).

Written responses provided directly by the interviewee to open questions are considered original literary works and copyright in this instance rests with the interviewee. When the answers are recorded on tape or video, the interviewee owns the copyright in the words and the interviewer can own separate copyright in the sound or visual recording. That is, it is possible for two separate copyrights to be created in one piece of material, in the same way that a producer owns copyright in a film but the writer owns copyright in the script spoken in that film.

The creator of a database owns the copyright in that database even though other people may own copyright in the separate records contained in the database. Under the Database Regulation protection applies only to a database where the selection or arrangement of the database amounts to an intellectual creation by the author (although the courts have yet to decide how to interpret this regulation). Copyright belongs to the creator, for example a market research agency, even in the case where the creation of the database has been commissioned or paid for by a funder (unless a written assignment of the copyright has been entered into – discussed below). Under Database Right, the creator has the right to prevent reutilisation or unauthorised extraction of data from the database whether or not they also own the copyright in the database or the records stored in it. This right lasts for 15 years. However, where the database has been made available to the public it is not an infringement of the database right for a researcher to extract and use the database so long as it is not used for commercial purposes and providing the source of the database is indicated.

Publications, to include derived datasets, based on the analysis of raw data by a researcher will, if sufficiently different from the original raw data, qualify as a different original work, and therefore a separate copyright, owned by the researcher. However, copyright in the original raw data remains with the original owner of that data.

Infringements and exceptions

There are certain rules to remember on what constitutes infringement of copyright.

To copy the whole or a substantial part of a copyright work, to issue copies to the public, or to broadcast the work, are all infringements, unless authority has been given by the copyright owner or the action constitutes 'fair dealing'.

It is important to understand that, just because a practice is widespread, this does not make it legal – it may still be an infringement of copyright.

Fair Dealing Exception

The 1988 Copyright Design and Patents Act includes provisions for what is described as *fair dealing*. This basically means that, under certain circumstances, an original work may be reproduced or published for the purposes of research or private study, criticism or review or the reporting of current events without infringing copyright. Academic research can fall within fair dealing. This may, for instance, allow brief extracts or quotations to be copied, without copyright clearance. It must be stressed that the exception only applies where the copying or publication of the work is 'fair'. The amount which may be copied is not specified but is usually interpreted as permitting the copying of one article from a journal or one chapter or 5 per cent (whichever is greater) from a book. If the copy is for personal use, one copy should suffice and it would not fall within fair dealing to make multiple copies. Electronic material is treated similarly, namely it is considered fair dealing to take one hard or electronic copy of part of an electronic publication (one article from an electronic journal or 5 per cent of a book or similar document) for private study or research. But it would not be seen as fair dealing to copy the whole document or put all or any part of that copy on a publicly accessible website without permission of the rights holder.

The EU Copyright Directive has recently tightened the law on fair dealing. It is now no longer justifiable to take copies for research if the research itself is for a commercial purpose. Copying now carried out for a commercial purpose requires prior permission from the copyright owner or payment of a copyright fee. The Copyright Licensing Agency has set up a 'sticker scheme' with libraries to collect fees – currently £9 per copy. The law only came into effect in 2003 and there have not yet been any legal challenges to clarify what constitutes a commercial purpose. However, the British Library and the Copyright Licensing Agency have together developed guidance which can be accessed at the British Library website (http://www.bl.uk/services/information/copyrightfaq.html). The guidance is set in the form of different scenarios but can be summarised as follows.

If a commercial research company is generating income from conducting research for a commercial or a not-for-profit sponsor, the purpose would be seen as commercial and the research company would need a licence to copy material for use in the course of the research.

If the sponsor of the research is a commercial company and intends to use the research to make money either directly or indirectly (and it is difficult to envisage any other outcome) the purpose would be viewed as commercial whether the contractor was another commercial company or a not-for-profit organisation (for example, a university). The researcher would require a licence to photocopy material for use in the course of the research. The position, however, is not clear in the situation where the sponsor is a government department or other public body.

Photocopying material to be used as background material for a book, where the author would expect to receive royalties, would probably be seen as commercial but probably not if the output was a scholarly article in a journal where the author receives no payment (even though the journal will generate income for the publisher). Similarly, photocopying material to be used in preparing a paper for an academic/learned conference would probably not be regarded as commercial, but would if the conference was a commercial event.

R&D in an educational establishment which is not related to any commercial venture would probably be viewed as copying which does not have a commercial purpose. Also considered not to have a commercial purpose would be an individual's own private research or study, which is unrelated to any commercial venture. Or any research that was undertaken on a genuinely *pro bono* basis.

The Copyright Directive relaxes the regulation of copyright of materials for visually impaired people. Not-for-profit bodies and educational establishments (so-called approved bodies) are now able to make accessible copies of copyright material in formats such as Braille, large print, electronic and on audio tape for visually impaired people without a licence. Researchers conducting research with visually impaired people may well wish to be aware of this change in the law and can obtain further details from the government intellectual property website.

Fair dealing also applies to databases. It was stated above that a publicly available database may be used for private study or research so long as the use was not for commercial purposes and the source was acknowledged.

If in doubt it is advisable to obtain authorisation of the copyright owner or to take legal advice rather than assume that fair dealing applies. Researchers in academia should also consult their institution's librarian, as it is likely that the institution holds a licence with the Copyright Licensing Agency which permits multiple copies for some purposes (invariably teaching) and a licence with the Newspaper Licensing Agency which permits photocopying of certain UK newspapers.

Provision for librarians and archivists

Certain librarians and archivists qualify for certain exceptions. Prescribed librarians and archivists are able to make limited numbers of copies of copyright works without the consent of the author as long as certain conditions are met.

Authority/licence

In many situations, social researchers may be able to rely on the fact that their uses of data are covered by authority, or licence, from the copyright owner. Authority can be implied from circumstances. The key consideration is whether or not the copyright owner created or donated the work with an understanding of what it would be used for by the researcher. If the answer is yes, then a licence may arise. If the answer is no, then the work should not be used without the authority being obtained.

For example, reproduction of an old questionnaire may amount to infringement. However, if the creator of the questionnaire would expect and would not object to its widespread use by researchers other than those who originally commissioned it, a researcher should be able to rely on that fact as an 'implied' authority.

In respect of interviews, in order to be able to rely on authority/licence, the interviewee should be given the opportunity to consent to the reproduction of substantial verbatim quotes by a researcher as publication by researchers in the absence of such consent is an infringement of copyright. This applies whether the words go down on paper, audio or videotape. Ideally, the interviewee should be informed at the interview of the broad purposes to which the data will be put. If this is not possible, then permission should be obtained after the interview. Obtaining agreement to reproduce a person's copyright work (their interview) is not the same as obtaining informed consent from subjects to participate in the research, but in practice when conducting research it is often appropriate to seek agreement to both at the same time. (Informed consent is considered in the next chapter which discusses ethical issues.)

Employers and copyright

Copyright in a work created by an employee 'in the course of employment' will belong to the employer. The key question is always, was there an employer–employee relationship present? If work is sub-contracted to another organisation or individual then there is unlikely to be an employer–employee relationship. As such, unless an assignment of copyright in writing is entered into, the sub-contractor will own copyright in the work created. However, even if there is an employer–employee relationship, copyright will still rest with the researcher (and not the employer) if the researcher was not directed by the employer to undertake the work and if the researcher undertook the work in his or her own time. In my time as a government researcher I found HMSO (who adjudicate on Crown copyright) to be most accommodating on this matter. Articles on methodology, which I wrote in my own time were ruled to be my copyright and not Crown copyright, even if the substance of the articles had drawn on, or had been informed by, knowledge and experience I had gained at work. The view taken was that I had not been instructed by line management to write the articles, and they were written in my own time, so copyright was, unambiguously, mine. Similar principles apply to works produced by academics who are employed in educational institutions.

Copyright in materials produced from interviews would normally rest with the interviewee (see above). However, if conducted in the course of the interviewee's employment, then copyright rests with the employer. Whether an interview is given in the course of employment will depend on a number of factors, although if given on the permission of an employer and in work time, it is likely to be given 'in the course of employment'. In such a circumstance the owner of copyright is the employer from whom any authority necessary should be sought.

Transfer of copyright

In all research projects it is important to be clear who owns copyright of the research instruments, the data and the final outputs as this determines who has the right to use what information and who needs permission from whom to make use of it. Having clarified the position it is possible to transfer copyright from the owner to another party and this practice is often helpful to the progress of research or is made a condition of the research. Securing the transfer of copyright is sometimes the best way of avoiding many of the potentially difficult issues set out above. This is because the owner of the copyright is free to use and exploit the work as they please, except for the moral rights of the original author, which may not be assigned. Moral rights may, however, be waived.

Copyright can only be transferred by a document in writing, which must be signed by the person making the transfer. Such a document is usually called an assignment. If copyright is being assigned, a waiver clause covering moral rights can be included in the assignment. Whilst a licence can be sought (see above), a licence is more limited than an unconditional assignment in that it does not hand over all rights. Moreover, a licence in most cases can be terminated on reasonable notice, unlike a transfer, which is final.

In some situations the researcher may want others to transfer their copyright to him or her. Data is a prime example, especially data emanating from interviews with research participants. Some researchers carry a standard form of assignment which is given to the interviewee to sign at the outset. It is for the researcher to judge when this is advisable.

When a researcher donates research materials to an archive, terms and conditions of access and use should be set out in order that the archive goes as far as possible to ensuring that any promises of confidentiality or otherwise are honoured. Providers of material to an archive may give a licence to use the material in certain ways. However, assignment to the archive is preferable. In all cases, the archivist should check that the donor is the owner of the copyright in the materials. For especially sensitive materials, access can be strictly controlled.

Copyright, it was stated above, is owned by the original creator of the work or his or her employer if created as part of their employment. Where does this leave funders of research who may feel that having commissioned the work they are entitled to some form of ownership and say in how the work is to be disseminated? Go back twenty years or more and this issue did indeed create difficulties, but standard conditions of contracts have been amended to clarify the position.

Most major government departments now include a condition in their contract that 'The copyright in all reports and materials arising out of the performance of the contract will be vested in the Crown'. (The major exception is the Department of Health, which allows the researcher to retain intellectual property rights – and by implication copyright.) The condition adopted by the majority gives those departments the authority to be the first to publish the findings of the research. However, the contract states elsewhere that the department will always attribute authorship to the researchers and not unreasonably withhold the authors from writing subsequent academic papers and articles based on the research. The materials of the research includes data and databases created during the research and this enables the department to commission others to undertake further analysis at some later date or to make the data more generally available if it so wishes.

Not all funders of research insist on owning the copyright of works emanating from projects they sponsor. It is the ESRC's policy not to seek ownership but for grant holders to retain copyright in the work they undertake and in the reports they create.

Most small charities will themselves expect to disseminate the findings of any research they fund (as often the reason for commissioning the research was to help them highlight or publicise a particular social problem). However, from my experience, they are not always aware of the legal implications and their contracts certainly do not address copyright. In contrast, the large charitable funders do recognise and understand the legal position. The Project Funding Agreement of the Joseph Rowntree Foundation makes clear that the copyright of the Summary Findings (a short summary of the research findings – referred to previously in Chapter 9) is assigned to JRF by the researcher. Copyright in all other materials, including the main report, remain with the researchers who created the work. However, under the Agreement, the researchers grant to JRF the right to 'reproduce, communicate and make available to the public' the main Project Report.

Researchers should take special care to clarify copyright when they enter into consortia, team up in informal ways with researchers in other organisations, or in cases where they engage freelance contactors to undertake some of the work. In such arrangements, who owns what? Problems can arise later over who has access to the data, who has the right to publish articles reporting the findings of the research and who the authors are. Obviously if everyone behaves according to the ethical codes discussed in the next chapter many of these potential problems are avoided. Nevertheless, it may also be worth anticipating the worst and entering into a formal written agreement at the outset.

Readers who have published articles in academic journals will be familiar with the requirement to transfer copyright of their article to the journal as a condition of publication. Authors are asked to sign a transfer agreement form prior to publication. The advantage to the publisher is that they have control over how the journal and its contents are reproduced and distributed throughout the world. They do not then need to seek agreement of every author whose article appears in the journal (some of whom may have died or their whereabouts not known) every time they want to make a specific arrangement. It thus gives the publisher the power to act if they suspect unlawful reproduction of the journal without making every author a party to the action. In return for the transfer, the journal promises to respect the rights of the author by always and clearly attributing the authors to the paper and by granting the author permission to reproduce and distribute the article for personal use.

Researchers should not assume that if an author or interviewee cannot be traced, it is safe to use the material in a way that was not envisaged at the time. It should not be assumed that copyright has expired on unpublished works because the author died more than 70 years ago. Copyright in unpublished works created before 1989 often lasts until 2039, regardless of when the author died. Hence, this can be a difficult area and researchers using old material are advised to take expert advice if in any doubt.

The internet

The contents of a website are no different in that they constitute copyright works and are owned by their author or creator. A recent EC Directive (which has been implemented in the UK by Regulations in 2003) harmonises the basic rights relevant to uses of copyright material in the information society. However, it is generally presumed that a licence to access the website or to download or print any part of the material is not needed as it is implied by the creator or operator of the website.

Confidentiality

The *duty of confidentiality* has evolved from court cases and, unlike copyright, is not governed by an Act of Parliament. The duty implies that confidential information handed over to a researcher can only be disclosed to others if the party giving the information has given authorisation. The duty also arises where the researcher has volunteered to keep the information confidential.

Authorisation to disclose should be obtained in the same way as authorisation under copyright. Indeed, if researchers explain as far as possible the details of the study and how the data will be used, consent from the subject will usually be sufficient to cover both copyright and confidentiality. Ideally, authorisation should be in writing but verbal authorisation can suffice where it is clear and unambiguous.

Where an explicit statement of agreement says that information is supplied on the understanding that it will be kept confidential or only used in certain ways, this may amount to a legal contract. This creates a contractual obligation in addition to the general duty of confidentiality. The contract does not have to be in writing.

If the interviewee requests anonymity, this must be respected.

Information given by an employee in an interview given during the course of employment should not be published unless the employer has given consent.

When material is being placed in an archive, lawyers advise that interviews be thoroughly anonymised unless interviewees have consented otherwise. Whilst this might distort data, to the point which lessens its potential for being used again, unless authority has been obtained, anonymisation is necessary where there is a duty of confidentiality owed. Further advice on archiving quantitative and qualitative datasets can be obtained from the Economic and Social Data Service (ESDS) at www.esds.ac.uk.

Regardless of how willing people are to be interviewed on the internet, this mode of information gathering does not mean that the need for confidentiality is waived.

An exception to the duty of confidentiality exists in cases where information is gained in an interview from a person who has been engaged in crime. There is no legal obligation in criminal law to disclose information uncovered in the course of research relating to criminal offences. However, if criminal proceedings are brought against the subject of the research, both the researcher and the interview records may be liable to subpoena by the court to disclose information gathered in the course of the research. Failure to disclose when legally ordered to can result in a criminal offence.

On two occasions during my time at the Home Office research notes were listed as material in a case (although, in the event the notes were not used). On both occasions researchers were examining the observance of powers contained in the Police and Criminal Evidence Act, 1984 (PACE) and involved interviewing arrestees brought into custody suites of police stations.

Researchers need to be fully aware of the possibility of being caught up in criminal cases, especially if they are undertaking taped interviews with serious offenders or victims of violence and abuse. The obvious way of addressing this potential problem is to explain at the start of the interview that the information given will be treated in confidence but if criminal proceedings are initiated the researcher may be ordered to make that information available to the court. Participants should be made aware of this before they reveal possibly incriminating evidence. (Although explaining this, the background to the research and the various research protocols to arrestees whose emotions are running high – in many cases fuelled by alcohol – can be challenging.)

Although researchers do not have a legal responsibility to report crime they do have a moral and ethical duty to report instances of malpractice or of physical and mental abuse. How does this accord with the duty of confidentiality and the assurances they have given to participants? Most would accept that that confidentiality should be breached where child protection is an issue. The Children Act, 1989, places a duty on local authorities to investigate cases or suspected cases of child abuse (s47(2)). Subsequent government inter-departmental guidance such as that produced by the Department of Health, the Home Office and the Department for Education and Science entitled *Working Together to Safeguard Children* (DoH *et al.*, 1999) calls on all agencies and 'the wider community' to work to protect children. 'Everybody shares some responsibility for promoting the welfare of children' (DoH *et al.*, 1999). Furthermore, all ethical codes of professional bodies acknowledge that confidentiality is compromised where children are in danger. The Barnardo's code states:

The limits to confidentiality should be explicitly communicated as follows: 'Whatever you have to say in this interview/focus group/questionnaire is confidential unless you disclose that you, or someone else, is in immediate danger of serious harm. In such a case I would need to report that to someone who might be able to help'.

www.barnardos.org.uk/resources/researchpublications/
documents/ETHICAL.PDF

Other questions need to be addressed. What constitutes 'immediate danger of serious harm'? To whom is the researcher going to report this? What should researchers do if they come across what they consider to be unacceptable behaviour which has the potential to harm but which cannot be regarded as immediate danger of serious harm? What about vulnerable groups other than children, should they be treated similarly?

There are no simple and straightforward answers to these questions. The researcher has to balance the integrity and scientific rigour of the research and responsibility for the welfare of the research participants. What can be avoided is being caught unprepared. It is important to develop a policy and lines of communication at the outset of the research, before fieldwork commences. This policy can then be conveyed to all concerned, including participants. A helpful starting point in developing an appropriate policy is the National Children's Bureau *Child Protection Policy*, which can be found as an Appendix in their *Guidelines For Research* at www.ncb.org.uk/ourwork/research_guidelines.pdf. Further guidance on research involving children and young people can be obtained from Alderson and Morrow (2004).

Ethical codes reviewed in the next chapter recommend that researchers consider whether or not it is appropriate to offer information about support services to vulnerable participants or to those who may have found the research a disturbing experience.

In studying some forms of malpractice or the misuse of power, researchers may feel that confidentiality should be breached in the public interest. The public interest is the only defence to not abiding by the duty of confidentiality. Israel (2004) reviews many of the difficulties and dilemmas that social researchers throughout the world have faced when investigating serious, organised crime and misuse use of power, such as international drug trafficking, armed robbery and child sexual abuse. Those dilemmas are not simply whether to disclose or not but how to negotiate or renegotiate a position throughout the research with participants, victims and criminal justice agencies while preserving the integrity of the research.

Confidentiality is most often considered in connection with qualitative research methods and records from interviews with research participants. However, confidentiality can be breached in quantitative studies if the aggregate data is disaggregated to such an extent that individuals can be identified. An example I recall is of a staff survey where the data were cross tabulated by age, gender, section and staff grade. This resulted in some cells having only one or two entries and it was not difficult for members of staff to recognise themselves or others.

Finally, the issue of confidentiality may be relevant when researchers are seeking to obtain sensitive information from third parties such as the police. The police or other third parties from whom information is sought may owe a duty of confidentiality to individuals who are the subject of the information. Not only would disclosure be problematic legally, the subsequent use of that information by a researcher may also be illegal.

Defamation/libel

The law of defamation/libel seeks to protect a person from untrue statements or inferences which harm his/her reputation. It is libel to publish such a statement. This situation could arise when an interviewee makes comments which are defamatory of another individual or – important to remember – of a company. If the material is to be put in an archive, the same consideration applies. It is important to note that a researcher, by publishing materials submitted by a subject, may be guilty of libel. Hence, it is essential that the targets of any potential defamatory statements be fully and properly anonymised, such that their identity is neither disclosed nor implied.

Data Protection Act

If you undertake social research which gathers personal information on identifiable living people then you will need to comply with the Data Protection Act. This applies whether the research is quantitative or qualitative, utilises administrative data or collects data direct from research subjects. It also applies whether the data is to be held on computer or manually.

The Data Protection Act (DPA) 1984 was passed in response to public concern about personal information held on IT systems. It gave individuals a right of access to their information. It also protected privacy and ensured information was accurate and used properly.

The DPA 1998 replaced the 1984 Act to meet the requirements of the European Union Directive. It came into force in October 2001 and retains a key element from the 1984 Act, that of providing individuals with a right of access to their information, but the new Act extends this right beyond computer records; it applies to all media used to record and process personal information including paper records, CCTV tape, and telephone recording as well as computer-based records. The new Act sets rules for processing personal information collected on living individuals.

Data protection principles

Anyone processing personal data must comply with the eight enforceable principles of good practice. These state that the data must be:

1 fairly and lawfully processed
2 used only for the specified purposes for which it was collected
3 adequate, relevant and not excessive for the specified purposes
4 accurate and up-to-date
5 not kept longer than necessary for fulfilling the purpose for which it was collected
6 processed in accordance with the data subject's rights
7 kept secure
8 not transferred to countries without adequate protection.

Definitions under the DPA

Personal data means data which relate to a *living individual* who can be identified:

- from those data, or
- from those data and other information which is in the possession of (or is likely to come into the possession of) the data controller.

Personal data covers both facts and opinions about the individual that affects that person's privacy, whether in his personal or family life, business or professional capacity. It also includes information regarding the intentions of the data controller towards the individual.

Sensitive data means personal data consisting of information about the data subject's racial or ethnic origin, political opinions, religious beliefs, membership of a trade union, physical or mental health or condition, sexual life, the (alleged) commission by him/her of any offence. Explicit consent from the data subject is required for processing sensitive data.

Data subject means a living individual who is the subject of personal data. The subject has the right to have a copy of the data held on him or her.

Data controller means a person who determines the purposes for which and the way in which any personal data are to be processed.

Notification

Personal data must not be processed unless the data controller has notified the Information Commissioner with descriptions of:

- the personal data being processed by (or on behalf of) the data controller
- the categories of data subject to which the personal data relate
- the purposes for which the data are being processed
- any recipient(s) to whom the data controller intends to disclose the data
- countries outside the European Economic Area to which the data controller might transfer the data.

In addition, data controllers must also provide a general description of the security measures taken to protect the personal data.

Processing means obtaining, recording or holding the information or data or carrying out any operation on the information or data, including:

- organisation, adaptation or alteration
- retrieval, consultation or use
- disclosure by transmission, dissemination or otherwise making available
- alignment, combination, blocking, erasure or destruction.

This definition is intended to be wide, and it is difficult to envisage any action involving data, which does not amount to processing within this definition.

Data processor means any person (other than an employee of the data controller) who processes personal data on behalf of the data controller. The data processor has no rights to amend the personal data, only to analyse or process it in accordance with the data controller's instructions.

Recipient means any person to whom personal data are disclosed, including anyone who is processing the data for the data controller (such as an employee or agent of the data controller or a data processor).

Third party refers to any person other than:

- the data subject
- the data controller
- a data processor or other person authorised to process data for the data controller.

Exemptions from the act

It is necessary under the DPA to state the purpose for collecting the data, as far as it is known, at the time of collection. Data collected for one purpose cannot lawfully be used for another purpose (see principles above). However, there is an exemption to this condition when using personal data only for statistical or research purposes. Data collected for one research purpose may be used for another research purpose. In addition, when using data for research the data may be kept indefinitely despite the fifth principle and access to their records does not have to be granted to subjects. However, the data must be kept secure and it must not be processed in a way that substantial damage or distress is likely to be caused to the data subject nor should the results of the research or statistics be made available in a form which identifies data subjects.

Enforcement

An Information Commissioner has been appointed to ensure that all organisations included within the scope of DPA conform to the Act. If any such organisation breaches the DPA, the Information Commissioner has a range of powers available. Ultimately, if he considers it appropriate he can issue an enforcement notice, which requires the data controller to cease processing personal data.

Implications for social research

First and foremost it is important that social researchers treat the Act seriously and comply with its provisions. Enforcement is becoming more stringent and ignorance is never a defence. But compliance with the Act is not a detriment to the research enterprise.

Large (or even small) reputable research organisations, higher education institutes, charities or public bodies will have a nominated data protection officer who takes responsibility for notification and the offering of advice to researchers within the organisation. Furthermore, those organisations will be registered and it is possible to access the organisation's notification at the Information Commissioner's website (www.informationcommissioner.gov. uk – click on Public Register of Data Controllers and follow instructions). Before embarking on a project, social researchers should consult their data protection officer and familiarise themselves with their organisation's notification. If the researcher's organisation does not have a data protection officer and/or the organisation is not registered they should speak to someone senior in the organisation about compliance with this requirement of the DPA. If the researcher is working on their own as a sole trader they should notify the Information Commissioner accordingly. It is possible to register online at the Information Commissioner's website or by downloading the form.

The DPA applies to collecting personal information on living individuals. Thus the Act does not apply to data collected about companies and other organisations and the deceased. Furthermore, the DPA relates to personal information collected on individuals, thus data already in the public domain is exempt from the Act. Data published in telephone directories, electoral registers, in the press or media, even publicly available court records would fall within this category and thus be exempt. What is personal information? It is generally accepted that a mere list of names or a record that a named individual occupies a certain position is not deemed as personal information. (But make sure that other personal information about that individual is not stored elsewhere in the system that can be linked.)

Social researchers should give serious consideration to the security of the personal data held. Is the IT system secure and is the data suitably password protected or encrypted? Consultation with the IT manager may be appropriate. Is the manual data locked away and who has access to it? Can a system be devised which separates the individual identifiers from the personal data?

The DPA legislation only covers data that *identifies* a living individual. Once any identifiers linking data to a person have been removed it no longer constitutes 'personal data' and is therefore not covered by the provisions of the 1998 Act. Hence, anonymised data is exempt from the Act as individuals cannot be identified. So consider anonymising the data at the earliest opportunity and if passing data to another organisation or collaborator it is advisable to anonymise the data first. Be aware, however, that simply removing a person's name may not be sufficient to anonymise the data as it is often possible to identify an individual from a combination of characteristics stored on the data file (e.g. date of birth, gender, ethnicity, occupation, postcode, etc.). This was discussed previously under confidentiality.

The requirement that the data subject has given his/her consent to the processing of personal data is generally assumed to have been met when the respondent completes a questionnaire or agrees to being interviewed. This also includes explicit consent (not well defined in the DPA) to the processing of sensitive data. If the data is being collected for the sole purpose of research there is a requirement to ensure that the respondents have a very clear understanding of how their data will be used before agreeing to be interviewed, and they must know that they have the right to withdraw from the interview at any stage. If, when gathering information for research and analysis purposes, it is made clear that the information will only be used for research purposes then there is no breach of DP legislation should the data subsequently be used for other research purposes – particularly if the data is anonymised. It is, however, advisable to include a note in the covering documentation that the information being gathered may be used in further research. This practice conforms to the good ethical practice of explaining fully to subjects the nature of the research and their involvement in it. If the subject is to be re-interviewed at a later date this should be made clear at the outset.

Particular care needs to be taken where different researchers have access to the personal data. This can arise in collaborations, when working in consortiaor when engaging subcontractors, agents or temporary staff. Which amongst the organisations is collecting, holding, processing, transmitting or disseminating personal data? Sharing data for research purposes is permitted but who is the data controller and who is the processor? There can be more than one of each. Are they registered and have they notified the Information Commissioner? Before entering into agreements about personal data or sharing data it is important to verify the other party's legality to collect or receive that data. Government Departments usually require written confirmation that the contractor is registered under the relevant parts of the Act (and it is possible to verify notification by searching the Information Commissioner's website). These problems are avoided if the data is anonymised before being shared but this is not always possible so it is important to clarify the situation at the outset and to take any necessary steps to comply with the law.

Further issues may arise in international collaborative research. Principle 8 states that data cannot be transferred to countries without adequate protection. Countries within the EU are accepted within the Act, the main contention arises when transferring data to the US, which is not seen by the DPA as having adequate data protection laws (although some would argue it has other laws that are more than adequate). If it is necessary to transfer personal data to the

US advice should be sought from the Information Commissioner (some guidance is at the IC website). Of course the problem is resolved by anonymising the data beforehand.

Under the DPA, data subjects have the right to see what personal information is held on them and to correct any errors. It was stated above that this requirement is exempt when data is being used for research. However, from an ethical standpoint, one would not wish to deny a research subject who has willingly participated in research the opportunity to access their record. It may thus be worth considering how such requests would be handled and whether this has any implications for the way in which the data is stored.

Like all legislation the details of how the law becomes interpreted and applied is shaped through challenges in the courts. Cases have come before the court and cases are to be heard in the European Court, which may alter, in due course, the interpretation outlined above. It is possible to keep up-to-date with developments as well as obtain further details from the IC website. The Market Research Society has also produced useful guidance, which can be accessed at www.mrs.org.uk and the MRS is working with the Social Research Association to produce further guidance for social researchers. The guidance will be published at both the MRS website and the SRA website in the near future.

Finally, related issues surrounding the legality of sharing data between different public bodies can arise when considering data protection. The law is complex but an informative guide has been produced by the Department of Constitutional Affairs entitled *Public Sector Data Sharing: Guidance on the law* (2003). It can be found at www.dca.gov.uk – and by entering the title in the search box.

11 Ethics in social research

In the formulation, design, conduct and dissemination of social research the research manager will face ethical choices or dilemmas, which will need to be addressed and resolved. There has been a recent upsurge of interest and a flurry of activity regarding ethics in research driven by two major concerns. The first relates to developments in the changing nature and growing complexity of social research, which poses new challenges. The increasing interdisciplinary nature of research is leading social researchers to collaborate on topics and with researchers from other disciplines such as health and genetics and thereby confronting them with ethical issues outside their previous experience. Of note here is the newly established Biobanks and the opportunities they provide for longitudinal research, linking socio-economic information with genetic data. International collaborative research exposes social researchers to laws and procedures of other countries. Technological developments, in particular the internet, may not raise new ethical principles but do raise new questions about how existing principles should be applied.

The second relates to concerns about procedures for vetting, approving and overseeing research and whether appropriate frameworks with sufficient responsibilities, powers and accountability are in place to regulate activity. These concerns are revisited later in this chapter when research governance and the role of ethics committees are discussed.

Reflecting these concerns, the ESRC has commissioned a study to develop new national guidelines, the Nuffield Foundation is mapping university practice in the scrutiny of research within universities, government social researchers are likewise considering their position. The Department of Health has drawn up a *Research Governance Framework* to set standards (including ethical standards) and the mechanisms to deliver those standards for health and social care research (DoH, 2001). The Department for Work and Pensions has recently developed its own approach to ethical issues arising in the kinds of research it funds (see Bacon and Olsen, 2003). In addition, reflecting the growth in comparative research across national boundaries, groups across Europe have collaborated in the RESPECT project to offer a common set of guidance to ensure a consistent approach in different countries.

Children's charities have taken a lead. In wishing to espouse the values and purpose of their organisation as well as safeguard the interests of children, they have drawn up ethical guidelines for research that involves children. Barnardo's and the National Children's Bureau have both produced Statements of Ethical Research Practice which they subscribed to when undertaking research, or expect others to subscribe to when undertaking research on their behalf.

Despite these recent developments there exists a broad consensus amongst social researchers as to what constitutes good ethical practice and this has been set out in Codes of Ethics or Codes of Conduct produced by professional bodies and learned societies within the social sciences. The purpose of these codes is to promote the highest standards of conduct by their members.

The codes promulgated by social science professional bodies and funders of social research are not, in the main, prescriptive. They do not dictate detailed procedures that must be followed. Rather they are presented as educational or aspirational, setting out principles and ideals and offering guidance to encourage members to act professionally and responsibly. The codes also serve another purpose by offering to members protection from external pressures to behave unethically. Having abided by the code, when placed under such pressure, members can expect their professional body to arbitrate.

The codes produced by professional bodies provide a good introduction and summary of the main ethical dilemmas social researchers will face and guidance on how to resolve them. Of course laws are in place, which serve to govern certain aspects of social research. In particular the law places a duty on employers to protect the safety and welfare of staff working on a project. (This topic was discussed in Chapter 7.) The previous chapter outlined the law relating to intellectual property rights (especially regarding copyright), the legal duty to preserve confidentiality of information provided on or by the subjects of research and the need to conform with the Data Protection Act when gathering and storing information. It is thus necessary to read these other sections of this book in conjunction with this chapter in order to obtain a full and rounded account of ethical and legal issues.

Codes of ethics

Working in the Sociology Department of a university and being a member of the British Society of Criminology, the Royal Statistical Society and the Social Research Association, I am obliged to be fully acquainted with the ethical codes promulgated by my institution and my professional bodies and to abide by those codes when undertaking research. Not surprisingly (and thankfully) the codes are very similar, although nuances vary and are influenced by the particular remit or focus of interest of the society or professional body. Not surprisingly, because all organisations share common values in the pursuit of social research and it would be surprising (and worrying) if they did not. When helping to prepare the code of ethics for the British Society of Criminology I read the codes of just about all other professional bodies, both in this country and overseas, engaged in social enquiry and I paid particular attention to the codes produced by the children's charities when undertaking research on young people. I have also drawn on developments within government departments, the ESRC and Europe.

All codes I refer to are accessible on the internet and can be found at:

Association of Internet Researchers: www.aoir.org/reports/ethics.pdf
Barnardo's: www.barnardos.org.uk/resources/researchpublications/documents/
    ETHICAL.PDF
National Children's Bureau: ww.ncb.org.uk/ourwork/research_guidelines.pdf
British Psychological Society: www.bps.org.uk (enter code of conduct in search
    box)
British Society of Criminology: www.britsoccrim.org/ethics.htm
British Sociological Association: www.britsoc.co.uk
Market Research Society: www.marketresearch.org.uk/standards/codeconduct.
    htm
RESPECT: www.respectproject.org
Royal Statistical Society: www.rss.org.uk (enter code of conduct in search box)
Social Research Association: www.the-sra.org.uk/ethics03.pdf
University of Surrey: www.surrey.ac.uk (click 'search our site' and enter in
    search box code on good research practice)

Readers may need to consult other codes, depending on their own professional backgrounds or the nature of the research in which they are engaged. It is not possible to cover every code here. The Social Research Association guide contains an extensive bibliography of publications on ethics in research.

Most codes are organised around a set of themes, which can serve as a checklist when considering the ethical implications of a project. Although covering much the same ground, themes are not uniformly classified within codes as they are not mutually exclusive but overlap and are interrelated. My own classification has been adopted here.

General responsibilities to society and the public

The Nuremberg Code (1947) formulated following the Nuremberg Trials, which took place at the end of the Second World War, and the Declaration of Helsinki, which followed in 1964 (and subsequently amended – see World Medical Association, 2002) established certain ethical principles relating to research involving human subjects. The Code and the Declaration addressed, primarily, issues around intrusive physical and medical research but did set out basic principles for all research. One general principle being that research should be undertaken for the benefit of society. Accordingly, the pain, disruption or at minimum inconvenience incurred by participants in research can only be defended if the research has the *potential* to improve conditions for others or at some later date. In many cases the research may not lead directly to positive outcomes, results are often 'insignificant' or 'inconclusive' but, even so, lessons should have been learned and understanding improved. An example here would be research to evaluate an educational programme for young people. The evaluation might reveal that the programme was of little value but society will benefit from knowing how to improve the existing programme or indeed whether or not to invest in such programmes in the future. The BSA code states 'members should satisfy themselves that the research they undertake is worthwhile'.

Researchers should also respect basic human rights and systems of values and to abide by the laws of the country in which they are based or where the research is being undertaken. The RESPECT Code highlights the importance of laws governing data protection and intellectual property rights (both of which are dealt with more fully in the previous chapter) but also employment laws and anti-discrimination laws. Researchers should not knowingly contravene human rights or the law and have a duty to make themselves aware of all the legislation that is relevant to their enterprise.

How is it worthwhile to be judged and whose rights and what laws are paramount? Conflicts of interest arise and competing concerns will need to be balanced. The subjects of social research are not always individuals but households, groups, communities, institutions and organisations. Much social research investigates power and the abuse of power, marginalised and disadvantaged groups and, in extreme cases, the lack of human rights, or may be based in countries where laws are considered unjust. While a particular study, or research collectively, may lead to general societal benefits, some sections may be adversely affected. I recall being involved in one study, which revealed the poor state of health for one minority group. The research did serve to increase awareness of the problem and to improvements in provision, but at the time some members of the group itself (but not all) felt that the research would reinforce negative stereotypes of them.

It is often difficult to predict what will be the consequences, and in particular the unintended consequences, of the findings of a research study and how they will be used. But, as the SRA Guidelines state:

> No generic formula or guidelines exist for assessing the likely benefit or risk of various types of social enquiry. Nonetheless, social researchers must be sensitive to the possible consequences of their work and should as far as possible guard against predictably harmful effects.

Promoting the discipline and responsibilities towards the discipline

Researchers have an ethical duty to promote the public understanding of their discipline and the status and standing of their profession. Mindful of public perceptions of statistics, The Royal Statistical Society states clearly at the beginning 'The Royal Statistical Society is a professional and learned Society which, through its members, has an obligation in the public interest to provide the best possible statistical service and advice'. Later, the Code states: 'Fellows shall seek to advance public knowledge and understanding of statistics and to counter false or misleading statements which are detrimental to the Profession'.

Similarly, being aware of the public concern about crime and political rhetoric that often surrounds it, the British Society of Criminology Code states:

> Researchers have a duty to promote the advancement of knowledge, to protect intellectual and professional freedom, and therefore to promote a working environment and professional relationships conducive to these. More specifically, researchers should promote free and independent inquiry into criminological matters and unrestricted dissemination of criminological knowledge.

In both cases the codes of the two societies link to their charitable aims. Both societies are afforded charitable status to promote the development of their disciplines with a view to encouraging open and informed public debate.

A duty to promote the discipline brings with it an obligation on researchers not to act in such ways as to bring the enterprise of social research into disrepute and thereby diminish the legitimate opportunities of future research for others.

As part of their professional responsibility, researchers should act with integrity towards other researchers, to support them and encourage the development of junior or new researchers. Conversely, 'whilst Fellows of the [Royal Statistical] Society are free to engage in controversy, no Fellow shall cast doubt on the professional competence of another without good cause' (The Royal Statistical Society Code).

Promoting highest standards of research

The public interest is best served and the standing of the profession greatly enhanced if research is conducted to the highest possible standards (within the constraints of time and resources). This places two obligations on researchers. First, researchers should use the most appropriate methodology available in order to maximise the outcomes of the research and to provide the best possible objective answer to the research question. Second, researchers themselves must maintain their own research skills and competencies by investing in their own training and personal development in order to stay at the forefront of their subject.

Researchers should strive to be objective and impartial at all times and the design of the study, or the method chosen, or analysis undertaken, should not compromise that objectivity or impartiality. Social research can never be entirely objective, itself being conducted within a social and political context. It is essential, therefore, that researchers reflect on their own values and beliefs and on how both might affect the research. Furthermore, researchers should reflect on the influences (if not pressures) they are under from their own institutions, research funders, colleagues and peers which might impact on their independence and objectivity, especially when formulating the research question or when publishing the findings.

The boundaries of social research are wide, methods are many and diverse and it is not possible, even for the most diligent and committed, to be expert in all areas and to stay abreast of all developments. Researchers inevitably specialise in both their substantive research areas and in research techniques. It is important that researchers acknowledge their limitations and do not lay claim, directly or indirectly, to expertise in areas they do not have. The BSA Code and the RSS Code expressly forbid members accepting work that they are not qualified to undertake. If offered work outside his or her direct competencies the researcher should decline and recommend someone more suitably qualified.

Obligations to clients, funders and sponsors of research

All codes recognise that researchers have a duty to the sponsors of research, in particular to abide by the conditions of any contract and to respect their unique relationship with the sponsors. In line with their responsibilities to society, researchers should not act in a way that brings research into disrepute with their sponsor thereby reducing the chances of other social researchers gaining the support of that sponsor. However, before entering into a contract the researcher should be satisfied that a condition of funding is not to comprise the objectivity and professional conduct of the research and the funding is adequate to complete the work. The researcher should 'seek to avoid contractual/ financial arrangements which emphasise speed and economy at the expense of good quality research and they should seek to avoid restrictions on their freedom to disseminate research findings' (British Society of Criminology Code).

Relationships with funders involve mutual responsibilities. Funders have obligations to researchers, especially, it might be argued, those that dispense public funds. At the commissioning stage, funders have an ethical responsibility to behave fairly and honourably, by not wasting potential contractors' time and by respecting the confidentiality and intellectual property rights of those that tender. Once the project is underway there is an equal obligation on funders to keep to the terms and conditions of the contract and not 'move the goalposts' part way through. The funder should also respect the professional integrity of the researcher who should not be put under pressure to produce outcomes that are most desired. Funders also have obligations towards the researcher when disseminating the findings of the research. These are revisited below.

In most cases the interests of the sponsor and/or the researcher are in accord – to undertake high quality, objective research and to make public those findings. However, should conflict arise, the Royal Statistical Society Code instructs its members that 'the public interest and professional standards must be paramount' and the Society will advise members 'and take action as seems appropriate' to resolve the conflict over professional standards or conscience.

Good management practice also dictates that roles and responsibilities are clarified at the outset and that agreements should be committed to writing. Contractual relations were discussed in Chapter 5.

Obligations to employers, colleagues and employees

The researcher's obligations to employers are broadly similar to their obligations to funders, namely to respect their contractual relationship. In addition, they should not bring discredit to their employing institution.

Research is often a collaborative venture and there is an ethical duty to promote equal opportunity and to actively seek to avoid discriminatory behaviour in the working environment. 'This includes a moral obligation to challenge stereotypes and negative attitudes based on prejudice' (British Society of Criminology Code). Junior staff, especially, who are more vulnerable and have fewer means for redress should not be disadvantaged. Other aspects of managing staff can be regarded as part of a general ethical duty to treat staff fairly and with respect. Included here would be creating a working climate and environment that enables staff to participate and contribute fully, taking steps to develop research careers and in ensuring the health and safety of staff. Some of these matters are covered by law and all were discussed in Chapters 7 and 8 so are not considered further here.

The University of Surrey Code specifically highlights the importance of leadership and the role of the principal investigator or group leader.

> 'Group leaders and other senior researchers should create a research environment of mutual cooperation, in which all researchers are encouraged to develop their skills and in which the open exchange of research ideas is fostered. They must also ensure that appropriate direction of research and supervision of researchers is provided.'

Researchers should, above all, fully and appropriately recognise the contribution made by all members of the team regardless of seniority. Researchers must not claim or present as their own, ideas of other colleagues or staff members. In any report or publication all contributors to the project should be cited as authors and the standard convention of listing contributors in alphabetical order should be followed unless it is clear that some have contributed more than others. It is possible that not to acknowledge a person's contribution may also be a breach of their copyright (see Chapter 10). The British Sociological Association has produced Authorship Guidelines, which can be found at www.britsoc.co.uk/Library/authorship_01.pdf.

Obligations to subjects

An important guiding principle emanating from the Nuremberg Code is that subjects should only participate in research voluntarily. Under no circumstances should they be coerced. In order to be able to exercise choice, the research and their involvement in it should be explained to potential subjects so that agreement is based as far as is practicable on 'informed consent'. Researchers, therefore, have a duty to explain as comprehensively as possible and in language that the potential participant can understand, what the research is about, who is sponsoring the project, why it is being undertaken, how long it will take to complete and how the results will be analysed and disseminated. If there is the possibility that the information given might be used at a later date or made available for secondary analysis by others, this too should be explained. Researchers should make clear the nature of the involvement that is required of participants (including any physical, social or psychological risks they face) and that they have the right not to take part, and if they do initially agree, that they have the right to withdraw at any stage. In other words the researcher should be open and honest about all aspects of the study.

To ensure that informed consent has been properly obtained, researchers are increasingly asking participants to sign a consent form. Following such a formal procedure may be necessary where the research is particularly sensitive or intrusive; where consent may be contested at some future date (for example that involving children or vulnerable groups) or where data is to be available in different ways to different researchers. When the subject of the research is an institution, public body, company or any other corporate entity, it is useful to have written agreement from someone in authority – although in practice this may have been covered in the initial exchange of letters when the organisation was first asked to participate in the research.

Where research involves children and young people, consent should generally be obtained from parents or guardians as well as from the child or young person. However, having obtained parental consent it is not acceptable to use this to exert pressure on the young person to participate. He or she must be free to make that decision independently. There may be situations where the general requirement to obtain parental consent might be outweighed by other considerations. The UN Convention on the Rights of the Child of 1989 stresses the rights of children to be heard on all matters affecting them. Respect for the rights of the child to make their own independent choices and decisions poses a dilemma if the child wishes to participate but the parent does not want them to. Similar dilemmas arise if the child wishes to participate but does not want their parent consulted over their participation. In balancing the respective rights of both parents and child, consideration has to be given to the objectivity and scientific validity of the research. A parental veto to their child's involvement in the research, or insistence in directing or controlling the nature of their child's involvement, may bias results, especially if family matters, personal relationships or sensitive subjects, such as illegal criminal or sexual behaviours are the subject of the research. In some research contexts there may simply be logistical or practical problems with obtaining parental consent.

The Barnardo's Code recognises these competing demands and states:

> The consent of parents or guardians should be routinely sought except:
>
> - where it is clear that participation in the research involves minimal risk (i.e. risks no greater than those in everyday life) and will not infringe the rights or impact on the welfare of participants
> - where parental/carer permission is impossible or would not protect the child or young person (i.e. where relations have broken down)
> - where the young people concerned are resistant to parental/carer consent being sought on the grounds of their right to privacy and confidentiality, and where the emotions and social maturity and particular vulnerabilities of the young people have been evaluated and the risks of participation are considered to be low.

For a more extensive discussion of the ethical issues involved when undertaking research with children and young people see Alderson and Morrow (2004).

Special consideration needs to be given to other vulnerable groups such as the elderly, those with learning difficulties, people in care or incarcerated in institutions. They may have difficulty understanding the nature of the research or be more suspicious, disdainful, anxious or fearful. Access to these vulnerable subjects is invariably through 'gatekeepers' (governors, wardens, relatives, carers, etc.) and information might be provided not by the subjects themselves but by those occupying a close relationship or a position of responsibility for them. In these circumstances the researcher will need to be sure that all reasonable steps have been taken to obtain informed consent. Where that is not possible and others are to respond on the subject's behalf, the respondent should not be pressed to disclose information that the subject would not want to be disclosed.

Informed consent may not be possible or appropriate in certain social research contexts. One situation is the secondary analysis of existing datasets stored in archives. In virtually all cases of this kind the data will be anonymised so the analyst will not know who is included in the sample in any case. However, on other occasions the researchers may be granted access to administrative data, such as criminal history data held in police, probation or prison records. Although it will not be possible to obtain consent, researchers should nevertheless reflect on the issues and consequences for the subjects of analysing the data. Researchers will also need to be aware of the legal issues surrounding confidential and data protection (both topics were discussed in Chapter 10).

Informed consent may also be compromised in observational studies, especially where the research is undertaken covertly. Such research may be justified, where to notify subjects that the observation is taking place may lead to alterations in behaviour and a distorted picture of the phenomenon being studied. It may also be justified in order to research secretive or illegal behaviours and activities where access to study would not be granted to social scientists. The British Sociological Association Code states: 'Participant or non-participant observation in non-public spaces or experimental manipulation of research participant without their knowledge should be resorted to only where it is impossible to use other methods to obtain essential data'. If consent has not been obtained prior to the research it should be obtained post-hoc where at all possible.

Researchers have a duty to honour participants' rights to confidentiality. Confidentiality was discussed in detail in the previous chapter; however, it is necessary for completeness here when setting out obligations to subjects, to emphasise the requirement not to disclose identifiable information given in confidence by subjects. It is also important to recognise the limitations to confidentiality. Where children are at risk of personal harm or where criminal proceedings are instigated confidentiality may be breached. Both situations were described more fully in the previous chapter.

Internet research does not raise any new ethical principles but may make it harder to observe those that have been identified already. To begin, internet research may involve obtaining and transferring data across national boundaries. Researchers need therefore to be aware of the laws pertaining to all the countries concerned and, equally, they need to be aware of the rules of conduct of their Internet Service Provider (including JANET – Joint Academic Network).

The Market Research Society has produced guidance on internet research. It points out that internet research takes different forms. It may simply be a means of sending, completing and returning questionnaires, the subject being selected and informed consent being obtained independently. The only issues to be considered in addition to those discussed above are the security of the data transmission. In other cases a visitor to a website might be invited to partake in research, by completing a pre-existing questionnaire or by means of an online interview. The website should contain full and detailed information about the study (along the lines discussed above) but in the design of the site it should be made simple for the participant to exit from the site at any stage and delete any information provided. Further issues that need to be thought through concern preserving the anonymity of participants, in particular the deletion or storage of email addresses and subsequent access to them. When emailing groups of participants it is important to ensure that each member of the group does not receive the address of other members.

Before undertaking observational research on the internet (such as entering chat rooms to observe communications between members) researchers will need to give consideration to what constitutes public and private space and the boundaries between them. Researchers should take particular care when engaging with children or other vulnerable groups via the internet. It is often difficult to be aware of a person's age or of their vulnerability from contact on the internet. Steps should be taken to obtain the person's age. If it discovered that the person is under 16, the MRS Guidance states that parental consent should be obtained before further information is obtained from the young person. Furthermore, it recommends that data collection should only be carried out within a protected environment (e.g. at home or in school) and in the presence of a responsible adult who is aware of the activity.

The MRS guidance also states that researchers or research organisations carrying out research on the internet must develop a Privacy Policy and that this statement must be made available as a link from every online survey. The statement essentially describes the research, what it is, who it is for, who is carrying it out. It emphasises that participation is voluntary and that respondents can withdraw at any stage and explains how security is to be ensured and gives guarantees that participation will not lead to unsolicited emails.

Researchers embarking on research on the internet will also find instructive *Ethic Decision-making and Internet Research: Recommendations for the AoIR ethics working committee*, prepared by Charles Ess and AoIR Ethics Working Committee, which can be found at www.aoir.org/reports/ethics.pdf.

Involvement in research might be a positive experience for many participants but for others it could be anywhere on a scale from mildly inconvenient, distressing or at worst physically, socially or psychologically harmful, especially to those who are vulnerable by virtue of age, infirmity, social status or powerlessness. There is an obligation on researchers to minimise the risk of adverse consequences to participants. (Researchers may wish to consider whether any form of support or referral to a support agency should be offered to those affected.)

Participants could well be institutions, organisations or corporate bodies. They may be the subject of the research, the gatekeepers or the suppliers of administrative data. If they are involved, researchers should be aware of the constraints they are under and not inhibit their functioning by imposing unnecessary burdens on them.

Having given of their time and having contributed information for the study, researchers should consider how they might feed back the results of the research.

Analysis and presentation of results

Researchers have a duty to apply the highest standards when analysing data and not to knowingly or deliberately bias or distort the findings. No false claims should be made of the results. In order that research can enter the scientific discourse and be subjected to professional peer scrutiny, researchers should make every effort to make their findings public and accessible. Presentation of the findings should include sufficient detail about the methodology and sufficient summary statistics so that others are in a position to make considered judgements.

Once in the public domain it is not always possible for the researcher to direct how that information might be used by others for their own ends. However, researchers have a duty to correct any distortions or misrepresentations made of the research.

Promoting scientific discourse and scrutiny also places a duty on funders of research to not unreasonably withhold or delay publication (other than on grounds of quality). In addition, funders should not dictate the form of the presentation of the results in such a way that would distort the conclusions or conceal information by which the conclusions can be judged.

Ethical review and regulation

Ethical principles are, more or less, universally accepted by professional and responsible social researchers, what is the subject of increasing debate is the mechanisms and procedures through which social researchers do, or should, gain ethical approval for their studies. The contrast with health research could not be more marked. Throughout the world medical research is governed more tightly and has been the subject of International Declarations and agreements, which were mentioned earlier. When undertaking health related research that involves individual NHS patients (alive or recently dead in NHS premises), their carers and NHS staff either directly or by accessing their records, researchers must gain approval from a Department of Health recognised research ethics committee (Department of Health, 2001). Medical research is viewed as potentially intrusive and harmful and the purpose of these committees is to ensure that participants are protected from unnecessary or unethical research. Ethics committees are concerned to weigh the potential risks and benefits of the research but also to be satisfied that participants are properly consulted and have freely given informed consent.

Across the UK there exists a network of Local Research Ethics Committees (LRECs), which reviews research to be carried out in its area. LRECs comprise twelve to eighteen members, of which one-third must be lay members in that they are not currently working in a professional capacity in the health field. A problem arose in the past when researchers wanted to undertake research across more than one local area, especially where national studies were proposed. Approval had to be sought from each LREC, which was not only time-consuming but led to different, even contradictory, comments from individual LRECs. To overcome these conflicts and to make the system more efficient, Multi-centre Research Ethics Committees (MRECs) have been established to review research that crosses LREC boundaries. At the same time, the Department of Health set up the Central Office of Research Ethics Committees (COREC), which governs LRECs and MRECs by formulating policy and setting standards. Information is available at its website www.crec.org.uk.

Social research in the UK (and much of Europe) by contrast, is not subjected to the same formal ethics review process. The codes of the majority of social science professional bodies place the onus on the social researcher conducting the research to abide by the code and to maintain the highest ethical standards. In social research the emphasis is on self regulation (except, of course, where it overlaps the boundary with health research – for example, surveys of dental health, care in the community or studies of patients' views of the health service provided to them – when it would fall under the aegis of a LREC or MREC). Amongst social scientists, psychologists have been the most proactive in seeking advice from ethics committees. The Social Research Association is an exception amongst social science professional bodies in promoting the establishment and use of ethics committees 'where they do not exist researchers should consider the establishment of ethics committees and the formal checks and safeguards to be gained from using them' (SRA Code, p. 41).

The question sometimes asked is whether all social research should be dealt with in a similar way to health research and be subjected to ethical review by an independent research ethics committee. This issue has been discussed in detail by Kent *et al.* (2002).

Supporters maintain that independent review afforded by an ethics committee would counter the self interest of researchers and afford greater protection (by minimising risks of harm) to the subjects of social research. They cite the experience of North America where social research requires formal approval of a properly constituted Institutional Review Board (IRB), based at each university and other research institutes.

Many social researchers are concerned about following too rigidly the path set by health research. Ethics committees in health, it is claimed, are very much conditioned to the notion of research being a quantitative random control trial involving an intrusive intervention. Most social research does not conform to that stereotype. Much social research is not intrusive and harmful, and the fear is that certain forms of social enquiry will be ruled out. As currently constituted, would committees be qualified to consider ethnographic approaches or other methodologies prevalent in social research? Furthermore, IRBs in the US have been criticised for being more concerned with protecting the institution's interests than those of research participants or of the progress of insightful innovative research.

The counter argument of the proponents of independent review is that members of ethics committees for social research would be drawn, in large part, from the social research community, members who would understand, appreciate and be empathetic towards the approaches of social research.

The extent to which social research is intrusive or harmful is also contested. Social research often examines sensitive topics, such as a person's deeply held beliefs, traumatic experiences or deviant and illegal activity. Participation in research of this nature can be threatening. Thus while it is true that risks in social research are more likely to involve psychological distress or violations of privacy rather than the physical harm of medical research, they are real all the same, especially to those who experience them. Furthermore, inequities exist. Vulnerable and powerless groups in society have difficulty in exercising their right to choose, to give informed consent or to refuse to participate in research. Ethics committees could redress this inequality, it is argued.

Another major concern of the social research community is the additional delay and bureaucracy that is introduced by having to seek approval from an ethics committee, which may only meet quarterly. Certainly anyone who has had experience of dealing with ethics committees shortly after they came into being is scarred by that experience, especially if they needed to seek approval from more than one committee. It was these experiences that led to the Department of Health becoming more engaged, leading to the creation of MRECs and COREC. As a result the situation has improved somewhat. Nevertheless, it is still the case that subjecting all social research to independent scrutiny would certainly require the formation of resource intensive apparatus to process all applications, including many research projects which may not require such extensive scrutiny. Funders of social research and institutions employing social researchers have been grappling with the issue of how best to achieve a balance that ensures appropriate consideration of social research without implementing an over-elaborate and expensive machinery. What is needed is a level of scrutiny that is commensurate with the potential degree of risk or harm to the research subjects.

After extensive deliberation and consultation the ESRC published in mid-2005 its *Research Ethics Framework*, which sets out what the ESRC requires by way of ethical approval for research it supports. (The document is available at the ESRC website.) Applicants will still be expected to address ethical issues within their proposal (as mentioned in Chapter 4) but from January 2006, when the new procedures are to be implemented, applicants will also need to state what he/she considers to be the ethical approval that will be required for the project, and how that approval will be obtained. The ESRC does not require that ethical approval is obtained prior to submission. Peer reviewers will be asked to comment on the ethical self-assessment in the proposal. If the application is successful the host institution is then tasked with obtaining ethical approval (most often from its own research ethics committee). Funding will not be released until the institution provides the ESRC with written confirmation that the required ethical approval has been received.

Before concluding this topic it is important to point out that ethics committees, however titled, biased or constituted, only consider a research proposal at its inception. Having granted approval there is no check on whether the researcher (in the health or social research fields) behaves in an ethical manner thereafter. The research manager and/or funder needs to think about implementing procedures that ensure guidelines and ethical standards are being followed at every stage throughout the progress of the research. One possible option is to extend the remit of the Advisory Board or Steering Committee to include consideration of ethical issues alongside their more traditional role of considering the scientific, practical and logistical aspects of the project. Although, in practice, most Steering Committees would voice its concerns if it felt that ethical principles were not being observed. As part of its new framework, the ESRC is looking to institutions it funds to establish procedures for continuing ethical review during the life cycle of a project.

12 Summary

- A project is a defined piece of work, undertaken for somebody within an agreed timescale and budget, using specific resources for a specific purpose.
- Thus aims and objectives must be clear together with criteria to judge that the project has fulfilled its aims and objectives. Quality needs to be specified, time scheduled and budgets allocated.
- Research is creative, original and innovative, which can lead research projects to be risky, uncertain and problematic. Assume that anything that can go wrong will go wrong and then take steps to minimise risks.
- There are stakeholders for every project. Who are they, what influence can they exert? Stakeholders need to be on board.
- Research projects are usually undertaken by teams, assembled for the task. Success often rests on good team-working – working collectively and to a high professional standard.
- To make an impact, findings have to be communicated to those who should know of them and in a way that they can understand and use.

Twenty questions for the project manager

A project manager has to be able to answer 'yes' to the following twenty questions.

1 Are the aims and objectives of the project clearly defined?
2 Are the outcomes realistic and achievable?
3 Will the methodology answer the research question?
4 Is the methodology robust?
5 Has a detailed plan been drawn up?
6 Is the plan feasible and has it been validated?
7 Is the budget adequate and will it cover all costs?
8 Is the contract clear, comprehensive and acceptable?
9 Have all risks been considered and steps taken to minimise them and their effects?
10 Have stakeholders been identified and approached where necessary?
11 Will all aspects of the research be conducted to a high ethical standard?

12 Have all legal issues been addressed and resolved?
13 Does the team have the right mix of skills for the project?
14 Have team members been fully briefed on the project and their role in it?
15 Has appropriate training been arranged?
16 Will the team gel?
17 Have procedures been implemented to monitor that the project is undertaken to schedule?
18 Have procedures been implemented to ensure attaining the quality standards set?
19 Have procedures been implemented to monitor the budget?
20 Has a dissemination strategy been prepared?

If the answer to any of these questions is no, remedial action should be taken.

Qualities required of a project manager

Ultimately, responsibility for delivering the project rests with the project manager. He/she has to manage the work, the team and the external environment. It requires vision and an appreciation of the wider context for the work. The project manager needs to be enthusiastic and committed to the project and the team.

Have you got what it takes? Do you have the qualities which will enable you to:

- analyse and solve problems
- make decisions
- organise
- coordinate
- delegate
- negotiate
- influence
- lead
- motivate
- communicate.

You will also need professional and interpersonal skills, a willingness (and ability) to support others and to conduct yourself in a professional, ethical and fair-minded manner.

If you feel deficient in any of these areas, think how you might develop your own skills and competencies. Alternatively, consider how you might arrange the management of the project to compensate for your own weaknesses.

Above all, when embarking on a project ensure that you have allocated sufficient of your own time to the project so that you can deal appropriately and effectively with the many and varied issues that will arise.

Learn from experience. At the end of the project reflect on what went well and what did not. Consult widely (team members, stakeholders and research subjects) to get their perspectives on whether the project could have been undertaken more effectively and in what ways your own performance in managing it could have been improved. Draw on that experience when initiating the next project.

Remember, successfully completing a social research project is satisfying and rewarding. Good luck.

Bibliography

Alderson, P. and Morrow, V. (2004) *Ethics, Social Research and Consulting with Children and Young People*. Ilford, Essex: Barnardos.

Bacon, J. and Olsen, K. (2003) *Doing the Right Thing: Outlining the Department for Work and Pensions' approach to ethical and legal issues in social research*. www.dwp.gov.uk/asd/asd5/WP11.pdf

Bulmer, M. and Sykes, W. (1998) 'Introduction: the present state of professional social research in the United Kingdom'. In M. Bulmer, W. Sykes and J. Moorhouse (eds) *Directory of Social Research Organisations in the United Kingdom, 2nd edition*. London: Mansell.

Burrows, J., Clarke, A., Davison, T., Tarling, R. and Webb, S. (2001) *Research into the Nature and Effectiveness of Drugs Throughcare*. RDS Occasional Paper No. 68. London: Home Office Research, Development and Statistics Directorate.

Chapman, M. and Wykes, C. (1996) *Plain Figures, 2nd edition*. London: The Stationery Office.

Commission on the Social Sciences (2003) *Great Expectations: The social sciences in Britain*. Academy of Learned Societies for the Social Sciences: www.the-acedemy.org

Department of Health (DoH), Home Office, Department for Education and Employment and the National Assembly for Wales (1999) *Working Together to Safeguard Children: A guide for inter-agency working to safeguard and promote the welfare of children*. London: The Stationery Office.

Department of Health (DoH) (2001) *Research Governance Framework for Health and Social Care*. www.dh.gov.uk/assetRoot/04/01/47/57/04014757.pdf

Field, M. and Keller, L. (1998) *Project Management*. London: The Open University and Thomson Learning.

Gowers, E. (1948) *Plain Words: A guide to the use of English*. London: The Stationery Office.

Hart, T. and Fazzani, L. (2000) *Intellectual Property Law, 2nd edition*. Basingstoke, Hants: Palgrave.

Higher Education Statistical Agency (HESA) (2003) *HE Finance Plus 2001/02*. Cheltenham: HESA.

Israel, M. (2004) 'Strictly Confidential?: Integrity and the discourse of criminological and socio-legal research'. *British Journal of Criminology*, 44: 715–40.

Kennedy, G. (1992) *The Perfect Negotiation*. London: Random House.

Kent, J., Williamson, E., Goodenough, T. and Ashcroft, R. (2002) 'Social Science gets the ethics treatment: Research governance and ethical review'. *Sociological Research Online*, 7(4). www.socresonline.org.uk/7/4/williamson.html

Lee, R. M. (1995) *Dangerous Fieldwork*. Qualitative Research Methods Series 34. London: Sage.

Lockton, D. (2003) *Employment Law*. Basingstoke, Hants: Palgrave Macmillan.

Murphy, B. (2001) *Project 2000 Made Simple*. Oxford: Made Simple Books.

Nuremberg Code (1947) http://bmj.bmjjournals.com/cgi/content/full/313/7070/1448

Office of Science and Technology (OST) (1993) *Realising Our Potential: A strategy for Science, Engineering and Technology*. Cm 2250. London: HMSO.

Office of Science and Technology (OST) (2003) *SET Statistics*. www.ost.gov.uk/setstats

Pettinger, R. (1994) *Introduction to Management*. London: Macmillan.

Scottish Higher Education Funding Council (SHEFC) (2001) *Academic Research Careers in Scotland: A longitudinal study of academic contract research staff, their jobs and career patterns*. www.shefc.ac.uk/library/11854fc203db2fbd000000ed49b85576/researchcareersinscot.pdf

Social Research Association (SRA) (2002) *Commissioning Social Research: A good practice guide*. London: The Social Research Association. Also available at www.the-sra.org.uk

Spencer, L., Richie, J., Lewis, J. and Dillon, L. (2003) *Quality in Qualitative Evaluation: A framework for assessing research evidence*. www.policyhub.gov.uk/eval policy/qual_eval.asp

Tarling, R., Burrows, J. and Clarke, A. (2001) *Dalston Youth Project Part II (11–14): An evaluation*. Home Office Research Study 232. London: Home Office Research, Development and Statistics Directorate.

The Research Careers Initiative (2002) *Final Report 1997–2002*. www.universitiesuk.ac.uk/activities/rci.asp

United Nations (1989) *Convention on the Rights of the Child*. UN: New York.

World Medical Association (2002) *World Medical Association Declaration of Helsinki: Ethical Principles for Medical Research Involving Human Subjects*. www.wma.net/e/policy/b3.htm

Index

activities, of work 79–80, 88
Advisory Committee *see* Steering
   Committee
Alderson, P. 151, 166
Arts and Humanities Research Council
   (AHRC) 53
Association of Internet Researchers
   (AOIR) 160, 168

Bacon, J. 158
bargaining 71–2
Barnardo's 150–1, 159, 160, 165, 166
Big Lottery Fund 55
British Academy 57, 96
British Crime Survey 7, 11
British Library 144
British Medical Journal (*BMJ*) 39, 56
British Psychological Society 160
British Sociological Association 160, 161,
   163, 164, 166
British Society of Criminology 159, 160,
   162, 163, 164
British Standard Organizations 123
budgets 30, 37–9, 63–4, 65, 72, 91, 103,
   112–14
Bulmer, M. 8, 11
Burrows, J. 76

call-off contracts 31–2
Carnegie Trust 9, 55, 57
Central Office of Research Ethics
   Committees (COREC) 169, 171
Chapman, M. 132
charities 9, 10, 50, 55, 66, 126
Charities Aid Foundation (CAF) 55
Child Protection Policy, National
   Children's Bureau 151
Children Act, 1989 150
Churchill, Sir Winston 130

*Code of Practice for the Safety of Social
   Researchers*, SRA Guide 101
Commission for Racial Equality 14
Commission on the Social Sciences 1
Commission on Equality and Human
   Rights 14
commissioning research 28–49, 139–40;
   commissioning procedures 40–3
Commissioning Social Research, SRA Guide
   29, 38
Communications Toolkit, of ESRC 126,
   128
Community Research and Development
   Information Service (CORDIS) 54
competition 29–32, 39–43: forms of
   31–2; running a competition 39–43
Concordat, for the career management of
   contract research staff 96–8
confidentiality 15, 149–52: duty of
   confidentiality 149
contract 73–4
contract law 15
contract research staff 95–9
controlling *see* monitoring
copyright 15, 93, 94, 140–9; Copyright
   and Rights in Databases Regulations,
   1997 141, 143; Copyright, Designs
   and Patents Act 1988 141, 143;
   Copyright Licensing Agency 144, 145;
   Crown copyright 141–2, 146, 147;
   employers and copyright 146;
   European Union Copyright Directive
   141, 144, 145; Fair Dealing 143–5;
   infringement and exception 143–6;
   internet 149; ownership 142–3;
   transfer of copyright 147–9
Costs *see* budgets
Critical path 81, 84
Crown copyright 141–2, 146, 147